Hockey's Hub

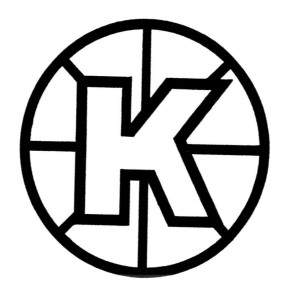

Three Centuries of
Hockey in Kingston

Hockey's Hub

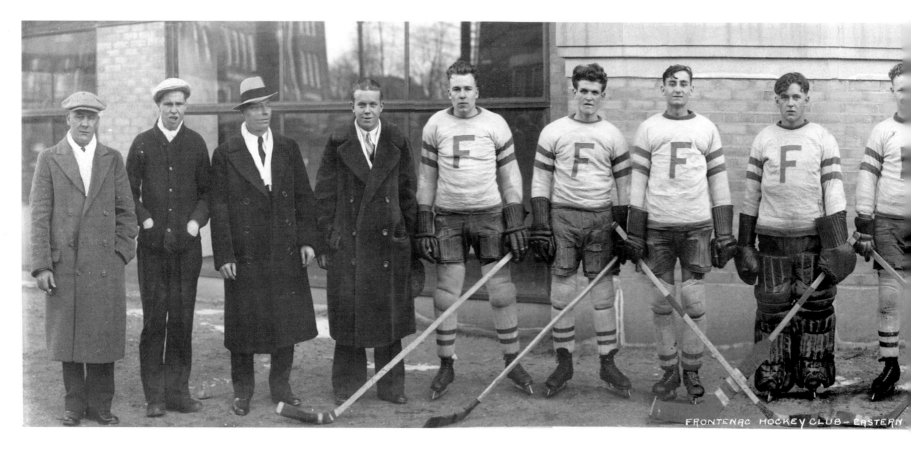

Kingston Frontenacs, 1932 Eastern Ontario Junior Champions. Team members line-up for the panoramic camera in front of the new Maple Leaf Gardens after tying Toronto St. Michael's 3-3. Reg Boyer, Albert (Boxer) Brown, Bill Steen, Spud Norman, Stew Langdon, Roy Covert, Wink Wilson, Ken Sharpe, George Pyke, Tip Roberts, Mickey Blake, John Nicholson, Bill Mooers, Rand Card, Art Casterton, Hugh Gibson, Oscar Simpson and Mr. Card.

Three Centuries of Hockey in Kingston

JUNIOR O.H.A. CHAMPIONS, 1932.

J.W. (BILL) FITSELL
and
MARK POTTER

Jock Harty (1893).

Text copyright © J.W. Bill Fitsell, 2003.
Photographs copyright © International
Hockey Hall of Fame and Museum, 2003.
Color photographs of Doug Gilmour and Jayna Hefford in color insert courtesy of the Hockey Hall of Fame.

The publishers acknowledge the support of the
City of Kingston, the Kingston Historical Society,
the Trillium Foundation, and the Book Publishing
Industry Development Program.

ISBN 1-55082-331-0

Edited by Doug Ford and Bob Hilderley.
Design and type by Laura Brady.
Special thanks to Ernie and Marlene Fitzsimmons and the Medical
Arts Department of Queen's University for scanning photos.

Printed and bound in Canada by
Tri-Graphic Printing, Ottawa, Ontario.

Published by the Quarry Heritage Books
(PO Box 1061, Kingston, Ontario K7L 4Y5)
in cooperation with the International Hockey Hall of Fame
and Museum (York Street at Alfred Street, PO Box 82,
Kingston, Ontario K7L 4V6, www.ihhof.com).

CONTENTS

Greetings *from* Don Cherry

KINGSTON HAS A PROUD HISTORY of hockey, starting with the Father of Hockey, Capt. James Sutherland, who founded our International Hockey Hall of Fame.

I was fortunate to be born and raised in Kingston—on Albert Street—and started hockey with Rideau Public School, then the Church Athletic League and Junior B with Max Jackson. Men like Max and Lorne Cook made hockey in Kingston.

The list of guys from Kingston who made it in the NHL goes on and on.

Make no mistake, Kingston is the cradle of hockey and I am proud to be a Kingstonian.

— DON CHERRY

Doug Gilmour, Don Cherry and Kirk Muller (Canada Day, 1993).

Foreword

KINGSTON'S HOCKEY ROOTS run deep. In fact, the very first written reference to the game of "*hockey*" appeared in the diary of a British army officer stationed in Kingston in 1843, more than thirty-years before the first "organized" game was played in Montreal in 1875. Kingston may not be the birthplace of hockey, but it is "Hockey's Hub" and there is no denying our significant contributions to the evolution and history of the game.

Name another city that can brag about four players who have scored Stanley Cup winning goals? (Bill Cook, Ken Linseman, Doug Gilmour and Kirk Muller). Can boast about Jayna Hefford, who scored the gold-medal winning goal for Canada at the 2002 Olympics. Or can lay claim to being home to hockey's oldest rivalry (Queen's University vs. Royal Military College).

You will also find the world's original hockey hall of fame in Kingston, the under-appreciated *International Hockey Hall of Fame & Museum*, celebrating its 60th anniversary in 2003. Captain James T. Sutherland fought to get the hall of fame for Kingston in 1943, but the NHL only contributed $7,500 to the building fund, reneged on a promise of an additional $30,000, and Kingston still didn't have a building when the NHL moved the Hall of Fame to Toronto in the late 1950s.

Finally in 1965, the International Hockey Hall of Fame opened at the corner of York & Alfred Streets. As the president of the IHHFM board of dedicated volunteers, it is a great honour for me to carry the torch passed on from Capt. Sutherland and the other great men who have followed, to keep alive this "little hall that won't quit."

To help celebrate our 60th anniversary, we have produced this book as a legacy to Kingston hockey. A very special thanks is owed to Bill Fitsell, one the world's pre-eminent hockey historians, for generously sharing with all of us a lifetime of research.

I know you will enjoy it.

— MARK POTTER
President
International Hockey Hall of Fame and Museum

Introduction

IN SPITE OF KINGSTON'S long and storied connection with Canada's National Winter Sport, no one has yet attempted to record a complete history. In 1987, in trying to unravel hockey's origins, I touched on the city's early contributions in my book *Hockey's Captains, Colonels & Kings*. Then in 1992, *The Whig-Standard* did the next best thing by publishing a supplement containing my record of the highlights of hockey from 1886 to 1992. Limited to ten pages and 16 photographs, *The History of Hockey in Kingston* drew favourable comments but didn't leave the readers with a permanent record for their bookshelves.

Thanks to the International Hockey Hall of Fame and Museum's initiative to mark the 60th anniversary of this shrine in a permanent way, that original history has been updated and expanded with numerous articles and photographs—and, voila, *Hockey's Hub!*

To me, the title seems to be most appropriate. Centrally located among the great hockey cities of Montreal, Ottawa and Toronto and convenient to the United States of America, Kingston has been pivotal in spreading the game to the west and to the south. Few Kingstonians realize that pioneer sportsmen from this city took the new game into Canada's West and into the American Mid-West, also introducing hockey into such eastern centres as Pittsburgh, Baltimore, and Washington, D.C. Other hockeyists who cut their first blade marks in the ice of the Kingston harbour or Jock Harty Arena demonstrated the game in New York, Boston, Cleveland and Chicago.

This puck diaspora was a "town-crown-gown" accomplishment, led by the city, the military and the university communities. Young Kingston men, impressed by the game introduced by Queen's University students and Royal Military College cadets, served as early administrators and contributed to the game's growth as players, coaches, managers, referees and executives. Capt. James T. Sutherland, "The Dean of Hockey," was the first of a long-line of pioneer players who dedicated their life to coaching, managing, officiating and administrating the sport throughout North America.

The Kingston contribution continues. As Kingston's No. 1 booster Don Cherry so colourfully tells all viewers of CBC's *Hockey Night in Canada*, few hockey games are played today without the involvement of someone who fired his or her first puck in Grapes's hometown, the old Limestone City of Kingston. The current commemorative print published by the International Hockey Hall of Fame and Museum, entitled *Kingston's Stanley Cup Winning Goals* and featuring Bill Cook (New York Rangers), Ken Linseman (Edmonton Oliers), Kirk Muller (Montreal Canadiens) and Doug Gilmour (Calgary Flames), epitomizes the exceptional contribution of local players to the National Hockey League.

Kingston women have also made splendid contributions as players, officials and administrators. Cookie Cartwright, Annabelle Twiddy, Rhonda Leeman-Taylor and Olympian Jayna Hefford take a deep bow!

Behind those notable leaders is a battalion of silent supporters—the generous parents and volunteers who make the game tick and solidify Kingston's reputation as a Hockey Hub.

This is not the definitive book on Kingston hockey, but it does contain most of the highlights over 117 years. Any errors or omissions are mine alone.

— J.W. (BILL) FITSELL
Historian

Capt. James T. Sutherland, The Father of Hockey in Ontario.
Capt. Sutherland was a player, coach, manager, and referee
who became a provincial and national hockey administrator.
He was the founder of the International Hockey Hall of Fame.

Kingston Frontenacs, OHA Intermediate Champions 1899. Kingston's first provincial championship team coached and managed by James T. Sutherland (centre row, fourth from left). Inset, right: Herb Reyner; Standing: W.H. Waddell, J.M. Shaw, A.M. Rae; Seated: J.K. McDowell, D.J. McDermott, Mac Murray, Sutherland, Charles Clarke; Lying: Richard Hiscock, Richard Wilson.

CHAPTER ONE

The Founding Years

ORIGINS

Where did this engrossing game of hockey come from? Who started it all?

The recorded evidence reveals that Halifax had a form of the game—one called "rickets"— early in the 19th century. Montreal, however, can be credited for "Hockey sur glace." It was played indoors, with rules, officials and a set number of players, 12 years before the first game was played in Kingston.

This was confirmed by a former Royal Military College cadet, W.A.H. Kerr, writing in 1893:

Hockey skated up into Ontario from the Province of Quebec. It was quite old before it left home, but it came slowly at first. Its earliest stopping point seems to have been Kingston in the winter of 1885-86.

The first match was played between Royal Military College and Queen's University. Some of the cadets, recruits of the previous fall, had learnt the game in Quebec schools

Royal Military College Hockey Team, 1888. Team members, mostly from Quebec and Nova Scotia, posed in their dress blues, not their hockey uniforms. The players, with RMC cadet numbers: Back row: E.M. McDougall (229), H.G.D. Campbell (212), W.A.H. Kerr (188), A.G. Bremner (182), E.A. Whitehead (209); Front row: A.N.J. Smart (211), W.H. Rose (202).

Queen's College Team, 1888. Seven young men formed the first Queen's College team: Sydney Harris, Walter Fleming, Hendry Leggett, Clem Burns, A.B. Cunningham, J.F. Smellie (centre) and H.A. Parkyn. They took the game to Toronto, Ottawa and Chicago.

and introduced it in '85 on the RMC bay [Navy Bay] where 'shinny' had held, until then, an uncertain foothold.

1886

SHINNY IN DISGUISE

"What is the game of hockey? It is 'Shinny' in Disguise!"

"Yesterday afternoon" (Ash Wednesday, March 10, 1886), *The British Whig* reported, "a hockey match was played on the Royal skating rink between teams selected from the Royal Military College and Queen's University.

"At intervals, before the game, people were heard to ask, 'What is hockey?' Few essayed an answer. Several of the players were tackled, but they said little. . . . Finally a cadet, who carried the rules upon a sheet of paper, said the game was very interesting.

"The players, seven aside: a goalie, a point, a cover point, a centre, 2 wingers, and the rover, lined up on the ice, with one referee and two umpires behind each goal marked by two posts in the ice. The point and cover point lined up in front of each other. The rover was allowed to roam over the whole ice surface . . .

"The game was started, and before the ball had been moving many minutes it was quite clear to many that hockey was only a funny name for 'shinny,'" commented *The British Whig*. "After playing an hour . . . Lennox Irving, of Queen's, who is an expert skater, poked the rubber through the cadets' goal."

This "rubber" was a cut down lacrosse bail, which was presented 47 years later to Queen's University by Mr. Irving, with this recollection of the famous goal: "There was a bandstand in the centre of the rink. I feigned a skate around the left side . . . but suddenly swerved up the right side and let fly a drive at the goal. The Cadet goalkeeper cleverly stopped the 'hexagon,' which bounded back, and the great 'I' struck the puck on its return and through the RMC goal, thus winning the game for us with the only score of the match."

At the time, sticks could be of any length "to suit the players" and no wider than three inches wide in any part, reported *The Gazette* of Montreal on January 8, 1886. This article gave the first description of the vulcanized rubber puck: one inch thick and three inches in diameter. The game was commenced and renewed by a "bully," a field hockey term for a face-off with the centres tapping the ice and their sticks three times before going for the puck. For a score, it had to be propelled between two six-foot-high uprights frozen in the ice, six feet apart—from the front side.

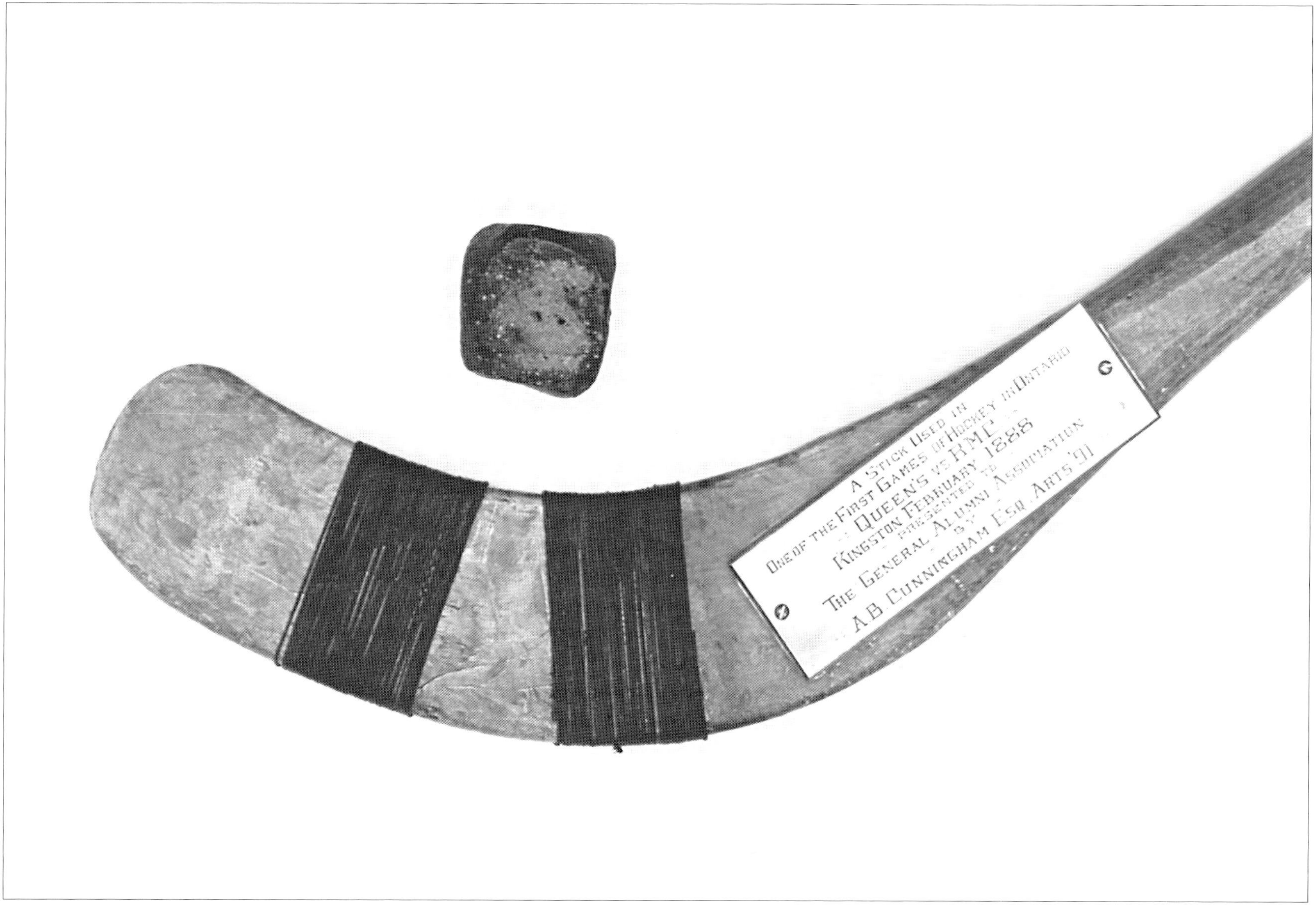
A Stick Used in
One of the First Games of Hockey in Ontario
Queen's vs R.M.C.
Kingston February 1888
Presented to
The General Alumni Association
by
A.B. Cunningham Esq. Arts '91

The Oldest Puck in the World. Used in the first Kingston game of 1886, this octagonal shaped, cut-down lacrosse ball is preserved at Queen's University along with the field hockey stick used in the 1888 match between Queen's and RMC, donated by A.B. Cunningham.

1887 A ROUGH GAME

There was still some confusion about the game and its rules when Queen's and RMC played the second annual match the following year.

"What is hockey?" asked *The British Whig.* "A sort of polo, excepting that a square piece of rubber is used instead of a ball, and knocked about by crooked stocks. The game is very rough and not very interesting to spectators."

J.F. Smellie, who later went on to play for Osgoode Hall and Ottawa—and eventually became a Supreme Court official—scored the first goal for Queen's. But W.A.H (Archie) Kerr of the cadets, came back with a brilliant effort.

"Kerr, who is a fine player, was loudly cheered," wrote Kingston's other daily newspaper, the *News.* "He has the science of the game down fine and it was amusing to see him, with the rubber before him, dodging past several of his opponents in succession." Kerr scored four consecutive goals, for a 4-1 RMC victory.

"Queen's students say they have very little practice at hockey, and were not fit to meet the cadets, who play the game frequently," commiserated the *Whig* reporter covering the game.

1888 REGI'S UNIQUE RINK

This year the annual confrontation between Queen's University and Royal Military College was no longer a sporting novelty, though both teams had their photograph taken in uniforms and suit clothes. Using only six players aside, instead of the usual seven, the teams met on Regiopolis Rink on William Street, which featured boards "one-foot high all-round." One Kingston paper dismissed RMC's 7-0 victory with the comments: "The cadets defeated their opponents easily." Queen's apparently couldn't believe the result and challenged for a second match in March. The result was the same, seven-zip!

1890 QUEEN'S FIRST COVERED RINK

After a one-year intermission because of poor ice conditions, Queen's and RMC resumed their rivalry in 1890. The cadets won 2-1 on Capt. Joseph Dix's outdoor rink—with foot-high boards—and then Queen's evened the series, with a 2-0 victory in Kingston Skating Rink, the second covered rink in the city's history.

"The first covered rink built on Queen's ground was a round-topped, tin-covered one that reached north and south where the [first] Jock Harty rink now stands. Strange to say the back end was at

Queen's University's Hockey and Curling Rinks. Constructed in 1891 on the present site of Miller Hall, the hockey rink hosted the first OHA games in Kingston, but was destroyed by fire in 1921.

Union Street while the entrance faced a narrow lane alongside the Old Medical Building," wrote Professor Manley Baker. Built by the late Senator Harry Richardson, the $10,000 project also accommodated curlers in a separate arched building alongside. The hockey surface, 75 by 150 feet, was lit by two arc lights, and spectators stood on a low 10-foot wide promenade on each side of the ice.

1891 ONTARIO HOCKEY (UNION) ASSOCIATION

The new building at Queen's gave hockey in the Limestone City a great boost, just as the Ontario Hockey (Union) Association was formed with three one-time Kingston residents —W.A.H. Kerr, J.F. Smellie and Capt. T.D.B. Evans—on the executive. For the first time, two teams were formed by city-born players, the Kingstons and the Athletics, plus the RMC cadets, were no match for Queen's in their handy rink. Some of the Kingston games were played on Capt. Dix's outdoor rink on the Regiopolis grounds,

This four-team group—Kingstons, Athletics, Queen's and RMC—has been touted as the first league in the world, but Montreal holds that honour as result of their four teams—Montreal Amateur Athletic Association (MAAA), Victorias, Crystals and McGill—playing a balanced 24-game schedule in 1888.

The Queen's team won the first the championship of the Kingston city league, and went on to eliminate Lindsay "with ease" in the first OHA series. Then the Tricolour team Queen's came up against the eventual champion—Ottawa—well-trained in teamwork as result of years of competing with Montreal teams. Queen's was defeated 4-1.

1892 INTERPROVINCIAL COLLEGIATE HOCKEY

The RMC cadets met and lost to McGill University in the first interprovincial, intercollegiate game, while Queen's met former Kingston players, Kerr and Smellie, in its OHA series with Osgoode Hall, which lost the championship to Ottawa.

1893 KINGSTON LIMESTONES WIN OHA JUNIOR TITLE

Kingston Limestones became the first local team to win an OHA championship by overwhelming Galt 12-1 in the Junior final. They were led by Dr. J.J. (Jock) Harty, who would be honoured later when his name was given to Queen's arenas. Queen's fell again to Ottawa in the OHA Senior finals but picked up valuable experience in a 4-3 loss to the touring Winnipeg team. The westerners, wearing shin pads,

Canada's First Junior Hockey Champions.

The Kingston Limestones, 1893
MEMBERS OF THE ONTARIO HOCKEY ASSOCIATION

BACK ROW—ED. SEARS, ARTHUR (DOC) IRWIN, HUGH WALKEM.
MIDDLE ROW—GORDON GUNN, DR. R. T. WALKEM, Q.C., D.C.L., PRESIDENT, "JOCK" HARTY.
BOTTOM ROW—GEORGE LOW, ROBT. SUTHERLAND. (MISSING FROM PHOTO "CHICKY" McRAE)

Queen's College Hockey Team, 1890-91. The legendary Guy Curtis made his debut on this Queen's team, dressed for the first time in their signature red, blue and yellow striped jerseys. Back: Sydney Davis, D. Herald (inset), M.E. Ferguson; Middle: E.W. Waldron, H.A. Parkyn, captain; Guy Curtis, Front: Robert Robinson, A.B. Cunningham.

introduced the "Winnipeg scoop," a swift and accurate shot on goal.

TWICE AS SWIFT AS AMERICANS

As the old year—1894— rang out, Queen's played a part in the formation of an intercollegiate league before hosting a touring United States college all-star team. Then Queen's matched the New Englanders at their own freewheeling, no-offside, "ball" game—ice polo—3-3 and whipped them 6-0 under Canadian "puck" rules. "The Canadians were twice as swift as their opponents and dodged with telling accuracy," reported *The New York Times*.

With Ottawa dropping out of the OHA, Queen's came to the forefront and won its first OHA Senior championship in 1895, with a 17-3 "miserable fiasco" against Toronto Trinity. Led by captain Guy Curtis, a model defenceman, and A.B. Cunningham, who scored five goals, Queen's challenged for the Stanley Cup, then open to all amateur teams.

Queen's "looked fierce, in their tiger striped jerseys," it was reported, but the team fell to the famous Montreal Amateur Athletic Association's Winged Wheelers 5-1, playing under Quebec rules on a larger Montreal rink.

THE MORNING GLORIES

Before the regular season started in 1896, the popular Queen's team followed newspaper advice, turned tourist and introduced the Canadian game to Pittsburgh. Then Queen's caught the train for Baltimore and Washington. In nine games, Queen's outscored its hosts 69-3!

Back in Kingston, a team of Queen's women students formed the Morning Glories hockey team. The Morning Glories of Queen's defeated the Black and Blues of the local ladies college in a unique game. "The clever stick handling of the players was a surprise," reported *The Queen's Journal* "and the rapidity of their rushes called for repeated peals of applause." In a return match before 1,200 fans, that raised $60 for the General Hospital fund, the Black and Blues squared the series. Leading the winners with two goals was Marguerite Carr-Harris, whose family name would become a by-word in Kingston hockey and military circles. The women, with skirts just above their boot tops, were complimented by *The British Whig* for playing brilliantly "free from rough house."

Kingston hockey received a set-back in mid-winter when the Queen's drill shed rink collapsed under the weight of a heavy snowfall.

Queen's Senior Team, 1893. Mascot/trainer Alfie Pierce reclines between crossed sticks under the foot of Captain Guy Curtis.

REMEMBER CAPTAIN CURTIS . . .

New York was the next place to conquer, and Queen's, with five Kingstonians in the line-up, blanked Yale, 5-0. The word of this victory, borne back to Kingston by telegraph, gave rise to the Queen's College song: "Remember Captain Curtis and the Conquerors of Yale!"

In 1897, the collegians finally had to share the championship limelight with a hometown team. Kingston Frontenacs, in their first year of organization, went to the final of the newly created OHA Intermediate series before losing to Berlin (Kitchener) 3-0 in Toronto. Jock Harty was the star of the Frontenacs, a team managed by Capt. James T. Sutherland.

QUEEN'S GOES FOR THE CUP AGAIN

Two years later the Frontenacs made no mistake in their second chance at the Intermediate championship. Capt. Sutherland's blue and white team defeated the famous Guelph Nationals 5-2 before 1,000 roaring fans, with referee Chaucer Elliott "ruling with a rod of iron," it was reported. This was the last local hurrah for legendary goaltender George ("Pinkie") Lamb who, like several teammates, was destined for ice action in the United States.

Queen's, with its fourth OHA crown in five years, took possession of the Cosby Cup and then won the new Robertson Cup. This led to a cry for the formation of a Canadian intercollegiate hockey union, but not before a challenge for hockey's greatest prize, the Stanley Cup. This time, the collegians faced "the haughty" Montreal Shamrocks. *The Queen's Journal* explained the team was well below par due to injuries suffered by Guy Curtis and Jock Harty in the recent series of games in Pittsburgh. Queen's lost 6-2.

27 TEAMS IN ONE TOWN

As the century turned the corner, hockey made one of its most valuable innovations—the introduction of the goal net.

Queen's, despite the return of Guy Curtis from New York, lost the Intermediate trophy to the Toronto Wellingtons 6-4 in a two-game, goals-to-count series.

After 15 years, Kingston could boast of 27 hockey teams, quite an accomplishment for a town of 18,000. Toronto, with 10 times the people count, could muster only 80.

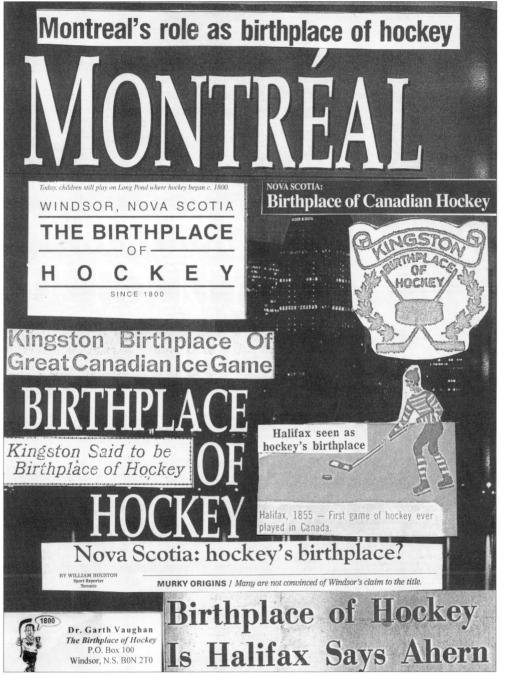

Montreal's role as birthplace of hockey

MONTRÉAL

Today, children still play on Long Pond where hockey began c. 1800.

WINDSOR, NOVA SCOTIA
THE BIRTHPLACE
OF
HOCKEY
SINCE 1800

NOVA SCOTIA:
Birthplace of Canadian Hockey

KINGSTON
BIRTHPLACE
OF
HOCKEY

Kingston Birthplace Of
Great Canadian Ice Game

BIRTHPLACE

Kingston Said to be
Birthplace of Hockey

OF

Halifax seen as
hockey's birthplace

HOCKEY

Halifax, 1855 — First game of hockey ever
played in Canada.

Nova Scotia: hockey's birthplace?

BY WILLIAM HOUSTON
Sport Reporter
Toronto

MURKY ORIGINS / Many are not convinced of Windsor's claim to the title.

1800
Dr. Garth Vaughan
The Birthplace of Hockey
P.O. Box 100
Windsor, N.S. B0N 2T0

Birthplace of Hockey
Is Halifax Says Ahern

The Birthplace of Hockey. Many communities, including Montreal, Halifax-Dartmouth and Windsor, Nova Scotia, have laid claim to this title. Kingston once vied for the honour but no longer makes a claim.

The Birthplace of Hockey Debate

"HOCKEY IS A CANADIAN game; its birthplace was Canada," the *Queen's University Journal* proclaimed in 1896. Yes, hockey is a Canadian game, no question. But where in Canada was the game born, invented, first played? This question has been debated for over a century now, with Montreal, Kingston, Halifax, Dartmouth, and even Windsor, Nova Scotia, all laying claim to being the birthplace of our national game.

While Montreal was referred to as "the home of hockey" as early as 1893—the first year the Stanley Cup was donated—the "birthplace" terminology was first born a century ago in 1903 in the City of Kingston, Ontario—Hockey's Hub. James T. Sutherland, a former player, manager, referee and a budding Ontario hockey administrator, started the discussion in January 1903, when *The British Whig*, Kingston's major daily newspaper, recorded his passing comment, "It is well to call to mind the fact that the birthplace of the game in Canada was the old Limestone City (Kingston)."

The *Toronto Star* soon after picked up the report and broadcast it nation wide, launching a public discussion that has been alternately raised to the rink rafters in fierce debate and let wane to a weak memory. For members of the local "Hot Stove

League," the 'birthplace' question has never disappeared.

Kingston's claim as "the birthplace" of the game gained impetus with the publication of the Sutherland contention in the *Canadian Hockey Year Book*, a highly illustrated history of the game published in 1924 by Joe King, then a resident of Toronto who later moved to Kingston. "It is generally admitted and has been substantially proven . . . that the actual birthplace of organized hockey is the city of Kingston," wrote Sutherland without offering factual evidence. The next year, 1925, *Maclean's* magazine added strength to the Kingston story with the challenging comment: "If there are any to dispute Capt. Sutherland's claim for Kingston as the birthplace of the game in Ontario, let them speak their piece now or forever hold their tongue." In 1927, the Kingston claim went international when the New York Rangers' program carried the birthplace statement in its official program.

Dartmouth, Nova Scotia, across the harbour from Halifax, entered the debate in 1936 with a mention as "the home where hockey originated." This belief was propagated despite a statement in a Halifax district rule book of 1903 that referred to the Upper Provinces—Quebec and Ontario—as "the home of the game."

The controversy really took off in 1941 when Capt. Sutherland—noting the opening of a Baseball Hall of Fame in Cooperstown, New York—convinced the Canadian Amateur Hockey Association to appoint a committee to study the origin of hockey in Canada—with no mention yet of establishing a hockey hall of fame, at the time. The popular 71-year-old Kingstonian, already crowned "The Father of Hockey in Ontario," was named to the three-man committee. The Toronto and Montreal members, weighed down with problems of wartime hockey, left the "origin" investigation to Sutherland, who had

1842
FEBRUARY
S M T W T F S
1 2 3
4 5 6 7 8 9 10
11 12 13 14 15 16 17
18 19 20 21 22 23 24
25 26 27 28 29 30 31

1843
January
S M T W T F S
1 2 3 4 5 6 7
8 9 10 11 12 13 14
15 16 17 18 19 20 21
22 23 24 25 26 27 28
29 30 31

Arthur Henry Freeling, age 23

Freeling Diary

On the 14th October died my uncle Sir James Lyon, Colonel of the 24th Regiment, having a wife and 6 children to lament him; how thankful I ought to be that my Father is not taken away from us and ourselves left to the precarious assistance & charity of friends & relations —

November.

Passes with no event of any moment to mark it —

December

Ordered on the 12th to Toronto to report on the road between the Fort & new Barracks at that place — Sleighed up in Stage on the 12th. Toronto night of the 13th at Mess with Story — 15th at 16th Mr Maitlands (daughter Kingston) and be 18th (D'Arcy) them to return to Sir

Began to skate this year, had great fun at hockey on the Ice —

— returned of the 21st I was by the hospitable people Barrows House — and had many games at Rackets. I was delighted with my visit, the pleasure of which was enhanced by the cordiality my old friends received me —

Rosedale, residence of Sheriff W. B. Jarvis

January — 1843 —

My Diary has now lived 3 years and a half — I myself am still spared; a living instance of God's mercy, while so many of my Relations are dying around me — Is permitted to finish this year? It that I dare hardly ask fit to die. and & Mother, Able, at all be happy; I hope I may nted —

with Airey a 4 in Hand drag (2 of my horses & his) to Napanee to bring into Kingston D. & Mr Maitland (sister to the Sampsons) and Miss Winslow distance 26 miles — started at 10, at Napanee at ½ past 1 — dined at Napanee, left at 4 came back by ½ past 7, having had a very pleasant drive — as the snow roads were rather heavy —

24th Drove Mr Sampson, B. Maitland & wife, to Napanee on their way to Toronto — 4 Horses as before — Airey and myself driving —

Began to skate this year, improved quickly and had great fun at hockey on the Ice —

Hockey on Ice, January, 1843. While stationed in Kingston, 23-year-old Lieutenant Arthur Henry Freeling (later Sir Arthur Freeling) recorded in his diary the first mention of hockey on the ice in eastern Canada: "Began to skate this year, improved quickly and had great fun at hockey on the Ice."

played the game since the 1890s and talked up its origin claim in numerous trips as a shoe salesman throughout North America.

The genial gentleman from the Limestone City launched a probe that provoked the greatest controversy in Canadian sports history. Its findings reverberate to this day. The report, presented to the CAHA in April 1942, was mainly the work of Capt. Sutherland.

When released in 1942, the pro-Kingston report drew a wave of criticism from Montreal and Halifax, where hockey officials pushed their claims with a vengeance. It was too late. Neither city had an advocate as energetic or as well liked as the genial Captain. With the establishment of this claim came another benefit to Kingston. In 1943, the Limestone City was chosen by the CAHA and the National Hockey League as "the most central site to erect a hall of fame dedicated to the greats of the game."

The joint decision did not end the "birthplace" debate, however. In fact, it intensified it. Sport historians and academics got involved in the heated discussion. In an eight-part series of articles, American historian Frank G. Menke of New York attacked the CAHA's Kingston-favoured report as a rather strange document— "a mass of conclusions unsupported by any facts."

"It is my opinion," wrote the author of *The All Sports Record Book*, "that it [hockey] originated in Halifax, was developed into a modern game in Montreal, then played in Ottawa and a short time later in Kingston."

"Hockey's home, without a doubt, is Montreal," chimed in McGill University professor E.M. Orlick. "It was conceived in Halifax but the game *as we know it* was really born in Montreal."

"No statements can be strong enough to condemn the hoax which the Kingston claimants have perpetrated on the sports-loving public of Canada," ranted Professor Orlick. "No amount of eye-wash, back-wash, or white-wash can convince any individual, who has seen the evidence in my possession, that Kingston has even the slightest shred of an historical claim, either to the origin of ice hockey or to the proposed Hall of Fame."

The Montreal claim was supported by a factual report of a nine-man game, played indoors at Victoria Skating Rink on March 3, 1875, and with line-ups and scores reported in the press the following day.

The Kingston claim was bolstered by a local historian's diary entry that referred to games of shinny— an unorganized pastime—played by crowds of 50 or more on the Kingston harbour ice in the 1840s. In 1975, an Ottawa sports archivist discovered an entry in a British army officer's diary for January 1843 referring to hockey: "Began to skate this year, improved quickly and had great fun at hockey on the ice." Although the quote was attributed to Halifax in *Sport Canadiana*, a chronology of various Canadian sporting references, I had first found it in 1975 and made a passing reference to the game of field hockey on the ice in *Hockey's Captains, Colonels & Kings*, published in 1987. However, the isolated "great fun at hockey" reference didn't prove that Kingston was the birthplace of ice hockey.

Nova Scotia's claim was not seriously considered until 1965 when a Haligonian published a scholarly paper with reports of "spirit-stirring games under different names— hurly, wicket, rickets—being played on frozen lakes in the Halifax-Dartmouth area as early as 1829." Thirty years later the word "hockey" was twice used by Halifax writers to describe similar stick-ball games on ice in Nova Scotia capital area around 1860.

Nova Scotia re-entered the debate in 1988, when King's-Edgehill School in Windsor published its bicentennial history. This pictorial essay by the late L.S. Loomer featured a quotation from

Thomas Chandler Haliburton's *The Attache, Part II*, published in England in 1844. A brief reference to schoolboys playing the Irish field game of "hurling" on the ice of Long Pond was turned into a *cause celebre*. Town boosters maintained that the few simple words were sufficient evidence to make the claim that hockey was played as early as 1800—when the author was four years old.

Like Pinocchio's nose, the Windsor story grew to great proportions, particularly with the publication of *The Puck Starts Here, The Origin of Canada's Great Winter Game, Ice Hockey,* as compiled by Dr. Garth Vaughan in 1996. The NHL and CBC-TV added credence to the claim by sponsoring events in the town, and the provincial government authorized the erection of highway signs declaring "Windsor—The Birthplace of Hockey."

This caused Montreal and Kingston hockey historians to cry "foul." Outside of vocal protests, nothing was done until May 2001 when the Society for International Hockey Research (SIHR), a 200-member body of hockey aficionados, appointed a six-member committee to investigate the Windsor claim. After a 12-month study, the committee reported that the claim lacked credible evidence. It was based, said the report, on a work of fiction—a writer's imagination. Windsorites were irate and criticized the process but offered little or no new evidence.

The International Ice Hockey Federation, based in Zurich, Switzerland, picked up the 18-page "Origins" report by the SIHR committee and announced that it would erect a plaque honouring Montreal as the place where the first organized game was played.

Then the focus of the debate switched to Dartmouth, Nova Scotia in 2002 when Martin Jones published an 118-page book, *Hockey's Home Halifax-Dartmouth, The Origin of Canada's Game.* "To suggest that the game of hockey which we know and love today did not start and evolve in Dartmouth and Halifax would be contrary to the historical facts that have been discovered to date," said the Dartmouth lawyer with reference to the SIHR report. "The suggestion that our area 'lacked a stronger hockey bloodline than Montreal' is untenable."

That is debatable. Dartmouth didn't move its lakeside game indoors until 1884, nine years after the first indoor game was played in Montreal. In 1889 when the Dartmouth Chebuctos played four exhibition games in Montreal and Quebec City, they faced teams from a well-organized association and found their own offside, lacrosse style of game—with strange goal markers—wanting. They lost all four games and soon adopted the Montreal game and rules.

At that time Kingston, with players from Quebec and the Maritimes, had been playing the Montreal game for four years and was on the verge of playing an important role in the organization of hockey in Ontario and its spread into the United States. "Hockey's Hub"—The Limestone City—because of its location and puck pioneers, including the founding of SIHR, has played a pivotal role in the development and lore of the game.

Long out of contention for the rights to hockey's parentage, Kingston now plays an important part as referee in the bestowing of "The Birthplace of Hockey" crown on Montreal or Halifax-Dartmouth. A Kingston writer discovered an 1891 article by a Haligonian that has provided the classic Canadian compromise to the birthplace dilemma. Having lived and seen various games in Montreal, Ottawa and Toronto, J. Macdonald Oxley discounted the Halifax games of rickets and hurley and the shinny of other centres as "merely local games" and declared Montreal the originator of "rink hockey." From there, the indoor game spread to Ontario and the Maritimes.

CHAPTER TWO

Into a New Century

The first decade of the 20th century marked the real dawn of professionalism for the fast-growing ice game. The large crowds of fans who attended hockey games at rinks built specifically for hockey replaced pleasure skating as the best source of winter sports revenue. The increased prowess, popularity and potential earning power of Canadian hockey players attracted the attention of owners of artificial ice rinks in the United States—and the exodus began. Amateur hockey players became professionals overnight.

Kingstonians were in the first wave of players being invited to "play-for-pay" in centres like New York and Pittsburgh. Among the "tourist" teams, Queen's Tricolour was the most popular. "Queen's received a bigger money guarantee than any other Canadian team," *The British Whig* boasted in January, 1901. However, the amateur purists in Canada, particularly in the fledgling Ontario Hockey Association, fought this "evil." The amateur vs. professional nature of the game remained a central debate for many years.

Hockey's face was changing, too. The game, now 25 years old, would see the first lines appear on its otherwise unmarked ice surface.

Marty Walsh. Pictured here wearing the red, black and white striped sweater of the Ottawa Silver Seven, this former Queen's player was the first Kingstonian to make it big in professional hockey. Walsh led the National Hockey Association in scoring for three seasons and was elected to the Hockey Hall of Fame in 1962. In one Stanley Cup game he scored 10 goals against Port Arthur (Thunder Bay).

George Taylor Richardson. The captain of championship teams for Queen's and Kingston, this prolific scorer and popular gentleman was elected to the International Hockey Hall of Fame. He joined the Canadian army at the outbreak of the First World War in 1914 and died in action one year later in France.

1901 KINGSTON EXPORTS

Four players, who learned their hockey in Kingston, became stars for the Pittsburgh Athletic Club in 1901: Herb Reyner, Mac Murray of Queen's University, and Jigger Robinson and George (Pinky) Lamb of the Frontenacs. The Smokey City was also seeking another ex-Frontenac, Stan Wilson, then playing in Buffalo. In a letter to the editor of *The British Whig*, an unnamed writer said Pittsburgh allowed visiting teams $400 just "for expenses."

While the four Kingstonians were apparently spared censure from the OHA, four London, Ontario players on the Pittsburgh team were "professionalized" and expelled by "The Iron Hand of the OHA." One of the true-blue amateurs was A.H. (Alex) Beaton, at Queen's University, who wound up six years as secretary of the OHA in 1901. A few years before, in 1898, this Maritime native wrote an article on early hockey that Nova Scotia historians use to this day to proclaim their province as "The Birthplace of Hockey." "Nearly 20 years ago," he wrote in *The Canadian Magazine,* "hockey, as a scientific sport, was introduced into Upper Canada from Nova Scotia, the latter province being the indisputable home in Canada of this game."

1902 RMC SUSPENDED

The OHA executive suspended the Royal Military College team because it played a game in Pittsburgh against a team with two of the London players who had been disqualified as professionals. Kingston Frontenacs, however, avoided such a suspension despite playing Pittsburgh PAC twice. Arrangements for the trip were completed before the OHA edict was announced. "Professionals may practise with amateurs and play friendly matches in the presence of spectators but must not play when admission money is collected," explained *The British Whig.* "Frontenacs will be quite safe playing in Pittsburgh as long as they don't associate on the ice with known professionals."

"Smokey City clubs are offerings all sorts of inducement," said *The Globe* of Toronto. "One of St. George's fast forwards was offered $40 a week to play there this winter—with transportation both ways."

1903 THE BLUE LINE

"Kingston does not and never did defend professional hockey alleged to be played in Pittsburgh," trumpeted *The British Whig*, "but it certainly admires Pittsburgh's openness to secret methods adopted by Toronto." Apparently, bank clerks from

Royal Military College Team, 1902. Players are "capped" in the tradition of British cricket and football teams. In the second last row is Robert Carr-Harris, a member of the Kingston family that sent eight sons to RMC. At the top of the "triangle" is Charles F. Constantine, who played with the Quebec City professionals and became commandant of the college.

Queen's at Duquesne Gardens, 1905. This rare "flashlight" picture of Queen's in their tricolour striped sweaters at left was taken on a tour of the United States. Queen's was the most popular touring team to visit this elaborate arena in Pittsburgh, Pennsylvania, where crowds of more than 5,000 attended games.

Quebec and Kingston transferred to Toronto to play in the "bank league." *The Globe* claimed that players, including four from Kingston, were being paid $15 a week —$5 extra for captains—to play hockey in Pittsburgh. *The Toronto Telegram* said Pittsburgh Street Railway Company apportioned $3,000 to each team and appointed a manager to disburse the money. "There is a continual agitation for an increase in salaries but there is little chance because of the inexhaustible supply in Canada at the standard price." What else is new?

In accordance with the new rules of the new Canadian Intercollegiate Hockey Union, a blue line was drawn across the ice between the goal posts "so that the goal judges [who stand on the ice behind the nets] could more easily discern a score." This marking, first used in a Queen's-Toronto Varsity opening game in Kingston, was the inauguration of many more lines to be added as the game developed. Ottawa added the goal line one year later.

Another idea, proposed by Capt. Sutherland, was to change the two 30-minute periods to four 15-minute periods. The OHA stuck with the traditional time, which gave only one intermission.

Queen's continued its Pittsburgh visits without the taint of professionalism and with much praise for its stars. "Guy Curtis is one the most finished hockey artists that ever strapped on a skate in Pittsburgh," said *The Pittsburgh Press*. "Jock Harty

is another oldtimer, who is a past master at the game . . . and an exceedingly speedy skater."

The Tricolour defeated McGill University, 7-0, in Montreal. The team, led by16-year-old George Taylor Richardson, lost later to McGill in the league final.

THE FIRST JUNIOR CHAMPS

Kingston's first championship of the new century occurred when the Frontenac-Beechgroves, losers to Toronto Marlboros in 1903, won the OHA Junior championship. The combined team, sparked by rugged George Van Horne and the Clarke brothers, Herb and Harold, whipped Listowel 9-5 by scoring five times in the second 30-minute period. Starring for the losers was a future superstar, Fred (Cyclone) Taylor, who drew a penalty for raising his stick above the shoulder.

Not to be outdone, Queen's became the second winner of the Canadian Intercollegiate Union title by defeating McGill 3-0 on a hat trick by rookie forward Marty Walsh. The Queen's rink was packed to the rafters.

FIRST LINE WAS SHORT

Queen's posed proudly in its striped tricolour sweaters under the title "Intercollegiate Champions

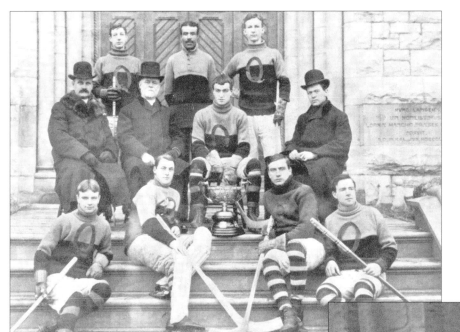

Queen's University Stanley Cup Challengers, 1906. Queen's challenged three times for the original Stanley Cup, in 1895, 1899 and 1906. Ottawa Silver Seven beat the 1906 Queen's team 16-7 and 12-7 in a two-game series. Back: Bill Dobson (RW), Alfred Pierce (Trainer), Hugh MacDonnell (Pt); Middle L-R: Prof. Nicol (Hon. Pres.), Principal Gordon, George Richardson (LW/Capt) Prof M.B. Baker (President); Front L-R: Vern Crawford (Cen), Richard Mills (Goal-Sec./Treas), Marty Walsh (Rover/VP), Eric Sutherland (Cover).

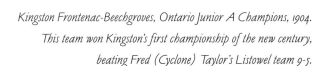

Kingston Frontenac-Beechgroves, Ontario Junior A Champions, 1904. This team won Kingston's first championship of the new century, beating Fred (Cyclone) Taylor's Listowel team 9-5.

of America" for a team picture in 1905, and went onto defeat the OHA Senior champions, the Toronto Marlboros, in a rink "blue with smoke." They had no trouble adapting to the new line drawn on the ice, three feet out from the net, that allocated space for players ahead of the play—and therefore offside—to take the puck as it rebounded off their goaltender. With future Hall of Famers Marty Walsh and George Richardson, the team was the most popular of the Canadian touring squads, attracting a record crowd of 5,423 in Pittsburgh's palatial Duquesne Gardens.

1906 JOCK HAD A SYSTEM

Restricted to student players only and using "the Jock Harty system" of playing, Queen's introduced jerseys with three broad bands of yellow, blue and red, and rolled to its second intercollegiate title in three seasons. Captain Richardson, who scored five goals in the 13-3 rout, asked the referee to impose no more penalties on the beleaguered McGill team.

Then it was on to the Stanley Cup, still an amateur challenge trophy despite reports of Montreal and Ottawa players being signed to cash contracts. Queen's opponents were the soon-to-be legendary Silver Seven, who were given silver pieces for winning the cup in 1905. The less-experienced students went down 16-7 and 12-7 in a two-game series in the capital. Queen's feat in scoring 14 goals against the champions was saluted on Page 1 of *The Daily British Whig* with this comment: "Quebec hockey is different from that played in Ontario. It is far more strenuous, particularly that played by experts like the Ottawas, who are a professional outfit from goal to centre."

1907 HOCKEY ON THE GRASS

This year was notable in that indoor hockey was introduced to Kingston at the Young Men's Christian Association (YMCA). This was the first local report of a game better known as field or grass hockey. Up until this time Kingston had only known ice hockey.

1908 PWORS WERE WINNERS

The 14th Regiment (Princess of Wales' Own Regiment) senior team, runner-up to Stratford in the 1907 Senior finals, turned the tables in 1908, thanks to the prowess of ex-Queen's winger Richardson and a new recruit from the RCHA, Art Bernier, a future Les Canadien. The soldiers took the Ontario championship 13-9 on the round, despite the loss of Marty Walsh to the Ottawa professionals. The tricky centreman made an immedi-

Queen's University, Allan Cup Champions, 1909. Queen's won the first Allan Cup title, beating Ottawa Cliffsides 5-4 in overtime in the championship game. Back L-R: Hugh MacDonnell (Pt), Alfie Pierce (Trainer), Lorne Pennock (Cover/Manager); Middle L-R: Principal Gordon, Bill Dobson (RW), R.E. McLaughlin (President); Front L-R: Gordon Campbell (LW), Greg George (Rover), A.M. Daniels (G), Vern Crawford (Cen).

Kingston 14th Regiment, 1907. While this team lost in the final for the Ontario Senior Championship, the following season, led by George Richardson and Art Bernier, they beat the defending champs from Stratford to win the 1908 Ontario title. Front row: Edgar Hiscock, W. Potter; Second row: Gordon Campbell, George Richardson, F. MacNee; Back row: John Powell, N. Steacy, Sam McCullough, Art Bernier, George Van Horne.

ate impact—scoring 29 goals in eight games, including seven against Montreal.

1909

THE ALLAN CUP DEBUT

With the Stanley Cup now dominated by the professional teams in Ottawa and Montreal, a handsome trophy for the senior amateurs of Canada was donated by Sir Montagu Allan to Ottawa Cliffsides. In the first challenge game, Jock Harty's fast-skating, backchecking Queen's team edged the capital club 5-4 after 15 minutes of overtime. The collegians' victory softened the blow for Kingstonians when the 14th Regiment lost the OHA Senior championship to Toronto St. Michael's 23-17 on the round. Cheers were heard in The Limestone City when Ottawa won the Stanley Cup, sparked by the play of Kingston's Marty Walsh with 38 goals in 12 games.

1910

MARTY WALSH STARS

This season, the town-gown victory schedule was reversed. The Frontenacs, managed by Capt. Sutherland, scored three goals in the final six minutes and edged Preston 8-7 on the round to win the OHA Junior championship.

Queen's, with the new Allan Cup proudly displayed in Kinnear d'Esterre's window, successfully defended challenges from Cliffsides and McGill but lost 5-4 to the OHA champion St. Michael's on St. Patrick's Day eve.

Students and townsfolk alike continued to bask in the glory of Kingston graduate Marty Walsh, who scored 31 goals in 15 league and playoff goals in the new National Hockey Association, the forerunner of the National Hockey League. For the third consecutive season he was the team's leading scorer.

Kingston Collegiate Institute Hockey Team, 1910. The junior team from KCI won the intercollegiate championship. Clockwise from left of cup: E.O. Sliter, J.L. Walsh, T.A. McNeill, E.P. Sliter, Lorne Larush, W.E. Goodearl, H.A. Stewart, William McCammon, Kinnear Reid, Leo Williams, A.T. Hatch.

Kingston Mic-Macs, Kingston Amateur Hockey Association Champions, 1908.

CHAPTER THREE

The Turbulent Teens

The third decade of organized hockey in Ontario saw Kingston's "grand old man," James T. Sutherland, play a prominent role as an administrator, while his favoured Frontenacs continued to vie for provincial championships.

The teens—1911-1920—were interrupted by the First World War, but the game survived, Sutherland became a military captain, and several local players developed leadership skills that would put Kingston on the map as a cradle for the new professional hockey league, the NHL. And with this new league, the number of players was decreased and the lines painted on the ice increased.

Queen's and the Frontenacs continued the tradition of spreading the game around the continent with exhibition games, both north and south of the border.

1911 HOCKEY MAD CITY

The Frontenacs, with cover point Alan (Scotty) Davidson in the forefront, ran roughshod over Ontario junior competition. They set a

Kingston Frontenacs, OHA Junior Champions, 1911. The Robertson Cup was draped in blue and white ribbons in front of manager James Sutherland and George T. Richardson after the Kingston Frontenacs again claimed the title of "Junior Champions of Canada." Front row: Ray Marchand and Leo Williams; Second row: N. Rae, Bert Hunt, George Richardson, James Sutherland, D.J. Dowsley, Alan Davison (Captain), Leo Millan; Third row: Reg Boyer, Sam McCullough, Jim Sutherland, Jack Cousins Jr. (Supreme Rooter), John Powell, William McCammon.

record in humiliating Picton 32-2, with Bert Hunt scoring 10 times. Led by the five-goal effort of Bouncer Brouse and a hat trick by Leo Milan, Kingston won 16-5 on home ice to win the round over Orillia 21-10.

"Not in the history of the games has Kingston been so hockey mad," proclaimed *The Daily British Whig*. Eighteen hundred people squeezed into the covered rink and 1,000 were turned away as Kingston repeated as OHA Junior champions. The Frontenacs went on to wallop the Quebec champions, the Montreal AAA, who were coached by Kingston's E.S. (Chaucer) Elliott, 14-4 and claimed the Canadian Junior championship. The Frontenacs went so far as to declare themselves the Junior Champions of the World.

Sutherland and the Frontenacs had another reason to celebrate. Former colleague Marty Walsh scored three hat tricks—one in each period—and a near-record total of 10 goals in leading Ottawa to a Stanley Cup victory over Port Arthur.

1912 ONTARIO KEEPS THE ROVER

Six-man hockey, created by dropping the rover—or "quarterback"—was introduced by the NHA, but the OHA stuck to the seven-man game.

Kingston Frontenacs, inspired by the coaching and prodding of Capt. Sutherland and the excep-

tional play of George Richardson, continued to be a force in OHA Senior circles. The blue-and-white sweatered squad swept eastern competition without a loss until the finals when they lost 13-4 to Eaton's in Toronto and were ousted on total goals despite an 8-3 win in Kingston. That was the city's last trip of the decade to the provincial final.

1913 ICE MADE BY MAN

The OHA season was extended by a few weeks when Toronto installed artificial ice—the first in eastern Canada. Kingston still had 10 years' more play on natural ice. The Frontenacs headed in the opposite direction —Boston—for exhibitions on artificial ice, where they beat the Pilgrims but fell to the Athletics.

After two terms on the OHA executive, Capt. Sutherland moved into the second vice-president's chair. One of the first pieces of legislation was to replace the three-foot line with a 10-foot line. This allowed defending players ahead of the puck to take a rebound off their own goaltender without being ruled offside.

1914 TWENTY-MINUTE PERIODS

As first vice-president, Capt. Sutherland saw one of his favourite projects, shorter periods, come into

Bath Road Beavers and Glenburnie Senior Hockey Team. Frontenac County village teams competed in the Kingston City League. The Bath Road Beavers (below) were the Kingston Township Junior Champions, 1910-1912. The Glenburnie 1911-12 senior team is shown here (right).

force. The OHA approved a change from two 30-minute periods to three 20's and limited overtime to 30 minutes.

Before the war started, Queen's Tricolour, coached by Jock Harty, toured Cobalt, Sudbury, Ottawa and Cleveland. The previous spring the Kingston college men won the intercollegiate title 4-3 over McGill. The game was marred by a dispute over the sounding of the referee's bell that allegedly wiped out a tying goal by the Montreal students with five seconds remaining.

1915 CAPTAIN MOURNS A HERO

With many of the older youth recruited for overseas service with the Canadian expeditionary force, high-school students moved into the OHA Junior picture. Kingston Collegiate Institute, with strong goaltending from a future Boston Bruin, Charles Stewart, won its group but lost out to the Lindsay midgets.

In OHA circles, Capt. Sutherland, now president of the Ontario body, decided that players practising with regular professional teams or given trials by such clubs would be considered professionals and banned from playing with amateur teams.

Cap'n Jim, in uniform, was deeply saddened by news from the war front. Capt. George Taylor Richardson, 29, one of the most brilliant hockey players ever developed in Kingston, died in France of war wounds, February 9.

1917 SCRAMBLING CURTAILED

The OHA extended the 10-foot "no offside" line out to 20 feet from the goal. This was made to speed up the game and prevent scrimmaging in front of the goal. Another innovation was the reduction of players from seven to six, conforming to the professional game. Two substitutes were allowed, necessitating the introduction of players' benches.

1918 KINGSTONIANS STAR WITH DENTALS

Neither Kingston nor army-based teams shone this year, but local fans had lots to cheer about. Toronto Dentals, with three Kingstonians, Charles Stewart, Rupert Milan and ex-Queen's player Willard M. Box, went to the OHA Senior finals against Kitchener.

1919 OHA DONATES THE MEMORIAL CUP

With the First World War over, Kingston again went seeking hockey laurels. The Millan brothers, joined by two future professionals James B. (Flat) Walsh and W.W. (Wally) Elmer, helped Kingston Frontenacs come within a few goals of defeating

William (Bill) Osser Cook. Tabbed as future star when playing for the Kingston Junior Frontenacs prior to World War I, after serving in France and Russia, Bill Cook starred for Saskatchewan Sheiks, three times winning the scoring championship of the Western League. He scored 33 goals in 44 games in his first year with the expansion New York Rangers and led them to two Stanley Cups. One of the game's greatest right wingers, Bill was elected to the Hockey Hall of Fame in 1952.

Captain Alan (Scotty) Davidson. After playing on two successive Kingston Frontenacs OHA Junior Championship teams, Scotty Davidson turned pro, leading the Toronto Blueshirts to the city's first professional championship and a Stanley Cup win in 1914. One year later he gave his life fighting for Canada in France.

Collingwood for the OHA Intermediate championship.

Following the battlefield deaths of two Kingston soldiers—Richardson and Davidson—Capt. Sutherland proposed that the memory of all Ontario players be honoured with the dedication of a new trophy. The OHA Memorial Cup, for Dominion-wide Junior competition, was instituted.

1920

DELIBERATE DIRTY PLAYING

Queen's became one of the first Canadian universities to hire a former professional player as hockey coach. Winnipeg-born W.R. (Nick) Bawlf, who had three seasons in the NHA and once scored five goals in one game against Montreal Canadiens, took over the Tricolour bench. In one of its first games under pro tutelage, Queen's and Varsity were accused of "deliberate dirty playing," so much so that future Hall of Famer Bobby Hewitson, who was refereeing, took off his skates and had to be talked into continuing.

Coach Bawlf renewed the traditional Christmas holiday exhibition excursions to the United States and coached the team to an 8-6 win over Yale before playing another contest with Harvard in Boston. "He's a magnificent find for Queen's," said a *British Whig* writer, who compared the coach to the legendary Guy Curtis and Jock Harty. Collegians and city fans crowded the covered rink, and Queen's cheerleaders, in white sweaters and trousers, cheered on the Bawlfmen. The talented mentor, however, moved on to Cornell University. He returned to Canada years later to coach the Olympic track team.

RMC's first indoor arena, reconstructed from two "flight sheds" from Camp Mohawk aerodrome at Deseronto, was officially opened on January 5, 1920 and named in honour of Sir Herbert Holt. The hangars had lots of length but only 68 feet in width, and the clearance between the ice surface and the rafters was only 18 feet.

Wolfe Island, 1920. Wolfe Islanders played between foot-high boards on the ice in Marysville Bay.

CHAPTER FOUR

The Building Twenties

The 1920s dawned brightly for Kingston pucksters and skaters with the opening of a new covered rink dedicated to the memory of famous Queen's player and coach, Dr. J.J. (Jock) Harty, who died in London, England in 1919. Located on Arch Street, the steel and metal structure replaced the old covered rink built, also on Queen's property, back in 1891. It was a vast improvement over the old Richardson rink and the Holt Rink constructed from two Deseronto airplane hangars at RMC in 1920.

The City of Kingston, mainly due to Queen's prowess, had accumulated 21 OHA championships in 30 years. The 1921-1929 decade, despite new facilities, would not be as productive in collecting provincial hockey silverware. However, Kingston-developed players were starting to make their presence felt in other leagues—for money and for glory.

Hockey was still an onside game in two-thirds of the ice surface. Passing the puck forward was permitted only in the defence zone. Kingstonians would soon see a move to the division of ice into three sections and more forward passing permitted as fans, particularly

Bill and Bun Cook, 1927. The Cook Brothers rated artistic coverage in New York as they led the Rangers into the Stanley Cup playoffs. They were purchased for $17,500—a remarkable sum in those days—from Saskatoon of the Western League.

Americans, clamoured for more goals.

1921 ADDING SCORING PUNCH

Queen's re-entered the OHA Junior series and went all the way to the final against the western winner, Stratford. The coach was W.P. (Billie) Hughes, also the football coach, who taught his hockeyists how to box. However, they lacked scoring punch in going down to Stratford 7-3.

1922 NEW JOCK HARTY ARENA

In the first Intermediate game played in the new Jock Harty Arena, Kingston Frontenacs, despite the megaphone coaching of Capt. Sutherland, lost 8-6 to Queen's, sparked by the play of Jack Woodruff and the Quinn brothers.

1923 QUEEN'S LADIES SHINE

Almost unnoticed was the entry of Queen's into the new Women's Collegiate Ice Hockey League. In three years, the tricolour ladies would defeat University of Toronto for the provincial championship and captured the W. Beattie Ramsay Cup.

In other action, Col. C.F. (Consy) Constantine, former commandant of Royal Military College, made a big hit playing goal for the Royal Canadian Horse Artillery team. Then 40 years old, the First World War veteran, had an impressive record on the ice rinks. He starred for Upper Canada College as a Junior, played rover for RMC's intercollegiate Intermediate champions and as a young artillery lieutenant in Quebec City, he had played in Canada's top hockey league. In 10 games against professionals, he scored 15 goals but lost his amateur standing.

In the first game of a now long-standing annual contest, Royal Military College of Canada defeated the United States Military Academy 3-0 at West Point—and a "war on ice" began.

1924 RMC VS. WEST POINT

The RMC-West Point series switched to Kingston's Jock Harty Arena, where the hosts gave West Point a lesson in offensive hockey, winning 10-5. Half of the cadet battalion was divided into two sections on opposite sides of the rink, with one instructed to cheer for the visitors. The RMC side had much to root about, including the hat tricks of the Carr-Harris brothers.

Hockey history was made this season when the Queen's-Canadian Olympic game was broadcast from the Jock Harty Arena by CFRC. The picked team won handily, 7-0, and went on to Chamonix, France, to outclass all opposition to win the first

Queen's Women's Hockey, 1925. A unique formation for their team photo, most of the players in this happy group wore tube skates. On the far right, the coach appears to be wearing a women's wig.

official gold Olympiad medal in hockey.

Hockey in Kingston received a seemingly devastating blow on a cold February night when the Harty rink was destroyed by fire. The loss was estimated at $98,672. However, before the end of the year, the arena was rebuilt and officially re-opened with a gala affair in which Queen's met RMC in an exhibition commemorating the first games played in Kingston in the 1880s. Jock Harty II was built at a cost of $95,000, complete with a refrigeration plant for icemaking, the first such plant between Toronto and Montreal. It could accommodate more than 4,000 fans with reserved seats for 2,000, rush seats for 1,500, plus standees.

1925

THE BLUE LINE ARRIVES

The OHA ruled that all rinks must have "a dark, distinguishing line" drawn on the ice 40 feet out from the goal line, where no offsides were called. Two seasons later the line was moved 60 feet out, giving the ice surface three zones of equal size. The name "blue line" was creeping into hockey language.

Kingston players continued to make headlines in other centres. Wally Elmer, a graduate of junior and intermediate teams, was a member of the Victoria Cougars, winners of the Stanley Cup. Lester Patrick's team had too much speed for even Howie Morenz and Aurel Joliat as the West Coast

champs whipped the vaunted Montreal Canadiens three out of four games.

1926

THE KINGSTON COMBINES

Kingston's junior hockey hopes and dreams almost reached the epitome of success this year. The Combines, wearing a huge "K" on a white jersey, included the best players from Queen's, RMC and the city, including three who would make their names in professional hockey—Carl Voss, Bill Taugher and George Patterson, not to overlook a future Montreal Canadiens owner in (Senator) Hartland Molson.

Coached by Lt.-Col. Tom Gelley, the Combines whipped Owen Sound 7-3 for the OHA Junior title and ousted North Bay, Quebec City and Fort William to qualify for the Memorial Cup final against Calgary. Kingston beat the Paul Thompson-led Calgarians 4-2 in the first game in Winnipeg but lost the second game 3-2. Under the old rules where the total goals scored in two games were tallied, Kingston could have suffered a one-goal loss in the second game and still won the Canadian Junior championship on goals. However, the CAHA ruled the national crown would be decided by a best-of-three series and Calgary captured the third games by a 3-2 score.

This year Kingston fans scanned the newspa-

Kingston Hockey Club, Eastern Canada Junior Champions, 1926. Three players went on to make their mark in professional hockey (George Patterson, Carl Voss, Bill Taugher) and one became president of the Montreal Canadiens (Hartland Molson). First row: C.R. McDowall, Hartland Molson, C.H. Smith, Y.J. Orford; Second row: George Patterson, Carl Voss, Bill Taugher, H.M. Reid, James McKelvey, G.B. MacPherson, Harold (Buster) Hartley; Third row: Thomas Gelley, James Sutherland, T.A. Kidd, E.J. Hartrick, T.A. McInnis.

Kingston Collegiate, Juvenile Champs, 1927. Crowned champions of Juvenile hockey, the first classification lower than Junior, this team featured goaltender/captain John Cunningham (holding the trophy), who later became president of the Church Athletic League. Left to right: H. Blomeley, K. Robinson, C. Roberts, M. McKee, J. Cunningham, D. Bews, P. Davoud, C. Cathcart, G.S. Stewart.

pers in following the exploits of two native sons, Bill and Bun Cook, with the newly franchised New York Rangers. Stars of the Western Hockey League, the Cooks, along with Frank Boucher, were a dazzling combination and made winners of the Broadway Blueshirts. Bill won the scoring title in his first season, with 33 goals in 44 games.

Meanwhile, former Kingston junior goaltender Alex Connell recorded his fourth consecutive shutout for Ottawa Senators in the NHL. And Kingston's George Patterson, after a short trial with the Hamilton Tigers of the Canadian pro league, jumped to the NHL and scored the first goal for the new Toronto Maple Leafs, formerly the St. Patricks.

1929
TRICOLOUR TOURS AGAIN

With Tom Gelley, the veteran RMC coach, recruited to direct Queen's, the Tricolour re-entered the OHA Senior series, where it was once a powerhouse and went right to the finals. Queen's lost to its old football nemesis, Toronto Varsity, 9-5, but the highlight of the season was a tour of New Brunswick, Nova Scotia and Prince Edward Islands.

Amateur hockey officials were keeping a close eye on the NHL's new rules, which permitted forward passing in all three zones.

1930
WALLY COACHES QUEEN'S

Wally Elmer took over the coaching reins and Queen's entered the OHA's new Senior B division and produced a strong performance. The Tricolour waved supreme before bowing to Hamilton Tigers 7-5 in the championship game.

Goaltender Charlie Stewart

Dr. Charlie Stewart. Kingston dentist Charlie Stewart starred for the Hamilton Tigers in OHA Senior hockey before he turned pro with Boston. In three seasons with the Bruins (1924-27), he recorded a 2.45 goal goals against average and 10 shutouts.

War *on* Ice: RMC *vs.* USMA

IN THE EARLY 1920S, two distinguished warriors of two peaceful nations who believed that "athletics possessed character-building qualities for officers in training" arranged for two teams of lightly padded young cadets to cross wooden weapons in a friendly game of ice hockey.

Brig. Gen. Douglas MacArthur was no longer superintendent of the United States Military Academy when a contingent of scarlet-coated Canadian cadets was granted special permission to enter the USA in uniform, but his co-supporter Sir Archibald Cameron Macdonell, as commandant of the Royal Military College of Canada from Kingston, Ontario, was front and centre in West Point, New York for the first contest in 1923. "Good old RMC," reported *The British Whig*, "came through with flying colours (3-0) and won honours not only for themselves, but for the whole country."

Over the next eight decades a unique, international intercollegiate competition blossomed from a gentlemanly, hands-across-the border exchange to an intense and colourful series of games that became labelled "war on ice." From a no-penalty tradition and host cadets assigned to cheer for the visitors in the early years, the series has evolved into an intense competition with rousing cheers and rinkside signs such as "Remember 1812!" and "Yankee Beer Sucks."

Right from the beginning, the annual game has been a "David versus Goliath" struggle. The United States Military Academy, better known as "West Point" and later labelled as "Army," had 1,200 cadets to RMC's 300 at the beginning and a 4,400-750 enrolment edge in 1990, but the Canadians had a distinct advantage in puck experience. After all, they had been playing Canada's National Winter Sport since childhood.

Canada's gentlemen cadets, who took on the nickname of "Redmen," went undefeated in the first 15 games against the Americans, who later adopted the "Black Knights" sobriquet, and lived up to it with spirited, football-style tactics. After 1937 when West Point installed artificial ice and improved recruiting of players from Massachusetts to Minnesota, the balance of power swung the other way.

It wasn't until the 1954, when RMC held a 17-6-1 edge, that officials, concerned with the rambunctious play, decided to call penalties. The first sentence was awarded to the West Point goaltender for a too exuberant slash on a Redmen forward. Nowadays, players are so intense and well-padded from helmet to shins, and attack with such vigour and vengeance, that penalties are adjudged in National Hockey League style and power plays are abundant. The series has been transformed from "the most sporting athletic event in the world," to "the most spirited."

Beside the crash and smash of bodies and boards, the game is a unique sporting spectacle both on and off the ice. The pomp and ceremony is equalled by few other sporting events. In the Kingston games, it is not uncommon to hear coronation trumpets greeting intermission performances and kilted dancers and highland pipes and drums performing with precision and agility.

Ironically, the series gained more nation-wide attention in its early, no penalty days. Hollywood discovered the attraction and made a movie starring the debonair idol, Robert Taylor. Appropriately, West Point won that year—1939. In the mid-eighties, Canada's national media discovered the series. One impressed TV commentator from Toronto was prompted to ask, "How come I haven't heard of it before?"

It's a remarkable feat that the series—played in 76 of the past 80 years and given that rules and interpretations vary in both countries—has been so continuously competitive and encouraged. The original Smith Arena at West Point had a massive ice surface, 232 x 90 feet that called for a much more wide-open, skating game than in Canada. Later reduced to more conventional size—200 x 85—the Americans were reluctant to install the centre ice red line that was introduced in Canada in 1943-44.

At Kingston, the early annual games were played at Queen's University's old Jock Harty Arena, where a breakdown in the artificial ice freezing plant caused the referee to remove a wavy, melted blueline—by throwing it over the boards! Since 1951, RMC has used the spacious, 200 x 90 foot ice surface of Kingston Memorial Centre and crowds of 2,500 to 3,000 have enjoyed the annual spectacle.

The early glow of sportsmanship that shone on the early games was replaced with an almost win-at-all costs attitude the years after the Americans matched the Canadian cadets in speed, skill, tactics and tenacity. Winning at West Point throughout the 1950s and '60s was a rarity for RMC. In the '70s and '80s, the Redmen returned on the short side of embarrassing double-digit scores.

Throughout the series, cadets on both sides have been coached by a cadre of dedicated and colourful men with long and

R.M.C., WEST POINT, HOCKEY GAME

COMMUNITY CENTRE, 8 MARCH, 8.30 P.M.

Royal Military College Redmen. A trio of cadets sprays snow in this 1954 promotional shot for the annual game with the United States Military Academy Black Knights at the Kingston Community Memorial Centre. Wearing cooperalls, the Redmen celebrate a goal against West Point during one of two victories for Coach Wayne Kirk's team in the 1980s.

short tenures—all of whom regarded the annual match between the two institutions as the highlight of the season. On the American side, there were Ray Marchand, a former Kingston, Ontario goaltender who survived the early years developing a competitive team at West Point, and the indomitable Jack Riley, who set a record for years of service—22. His will-to-win manner was succeeded by another intense, take no prisoner's coach—his son, Rob Riley.

On the Canadian side, there is an illustrious roster of coaches who have voiced the "Beat West Point" call. The Redmen have been led by Lt. Col. T.F. (Tom) Gelley, who was behind the bench in the 1920s, and extends through ex-pro Harry (Yip) Radley, Peter Carr-Harris, Major W.J. (Danny) McLeod, Dr. Wayne Kirk, Tom McKay, Jacques Tremblay and Andy Scott, to today's McGill-trained Kelly Nobes. Of later day coaches, only Tom Walton (one win and two ties in the 1970s) and the scholarly Dr. Kirk (4-2 in the 1980s), had a winning record, with the latter recording two wins at West Point.

After decades playing under the nickname of "Redmen," RMC switched to "Paladins" in 1997 and started to compile a better record in the annual series. Since carrying the crest of a 14th century European knight, the Canadians have played almost .500 hockey with two wins, three losses and a tie.

Whether the series has "strengthened the bonds of comradeship and international goodwill"—as proclaimed by sports editor Mike Rodden in 1950—is questionable. But there is no doubt that the on-ice clash of cadets from these two institutions continues to stir the blood and set standards for spirited, physical play and a never-say-die attitude.

And this outlook is not liable to change as long as RMC cadets respect their college motto—"Truth, Duty, Valour."

RMC–USMA SERIES STATISTICS

1923	RMC	3	USMA	0	West Point
1924	RMC	10	USMA	5	Kingston
1925	RMC	5	USMA	0	West Point
1926	No Game				
1927	RMC	7	USMA	2	Kingston
1928	RMC	8	USMA	2	West Point
1929	RMC	7	USMA	3	Kingston
1930	RMC	5	USMA	3	West Point
1931	RMC	7	USMA	5	Kingston
1932	RMC	7	USMA	1	West Point
1933	RMC	6	USMA	1	Kingston
1934	RMC	6	USMA	4	West Point
1935	RMC*	4	USMA	4	Kingston
1936	RMC	5	USMA	2	West Point
1937	RMC	4	USMA	1	Kingston
1938	RMC	1	USMA	0	West Point
1939	USMA	3	RMC	2	Kingston
1940	No Game				
1941	No Game				
1942	USMA	3	RMC	1	West Point
1943	1948—No Games				
1949	USMA	5	RMC	4	West Point
1950	RMC	6	USMA	4	Kingston
1951	USMA	4	RMC	2	West Point
1952	RMC	7	USMA	4	Kingston
1953	USMA	5	RMC	4	West Point
1954	USMA	5	RMC	3	Kingston
1955	RMC	3	USMA	2	West Point
1956	USMA	3	RMC	2	Kingston
1957	USMA	7	RMC	2	West Point
1958	USMA	5	RMC	1	Kingston
1959	RMC	6	USMA	1	West Point
1960	USMA	7	RMC	5	Kingston
1961	USMA	7	RMC	1	West Point
1962	USMA	3	RMC	2	Kingston
1963	USMA	9	RMC	4	West Point
1964	RMC	4	USMA	2	Kingston
1965	USMA	6	RMC	0	West Point

1966	RMC	8	USMA	3	Kingston
1967	USMA	9	RMC	1	West Point
1968	USMA	4	RMC	2	Kingston
1969	USMA	5	RMC	2	West Point
1970	USMA	3	RMC	2	Kingston
1971	USMA	6	RMC	0	West Point
1972	RMC	7	USMA	4	Kingston
1973	RMC*	4	USMA	4	West Point
1974	RMC*	4	USMA	4	Kingston
1975	USMA	2	RMC	1	West Point
1976	RMC*	4	USMA	4	Kingston
1977	USMA	11	RMC	2	West Point
1978	RMC	7	USMA	6	Kingston
1979	USMA	12	RMC	4	West Point
1980	RMC	5	USMA	2	Kingston
1981	USMA	10	RMC	5	West Point
1982	RMC	4	USMA	3	Kingston
1983	RMC	3	USMA	2	West Point
1984	RMC	8	USMA	5	Kingston
1985	USMA	6	RMC	4	West Point
1986	USMA	9	RMC	7	Kingston
1987	RMC	4	USMA	3	West Point
1988	USMA	4	RMC	3	Kingston
1989	USMA	3	RMC	2	West Point
1990	RMC*	3	USMA	3	Kingston
1991	USMA	11	RMC	1	West Point
1992	USMA	3	RMC	2	Kingston
1993	USMA	6	RMC	2	West Point
1994	USMA	6	RMC	0	Kingston
1995	USMA	6	RMC-CMR	1	West Point
1996	USMA	2	RMC-CMR	0	Kingston
1997	USMA	7	RMC-CMR	3	West Point
1998	RMC-CMR*	2	USMA	2	Kingston
1999	USMA	3	RMC-CMR	1	West Point
2000	RMC-CMR	3	USMA	0	Kingston
2001	USMA	7	RMC-CMR	1	West Point
2002	RMC-CMR	2	USMA	1	Kingston
2003	USMA	4	RMC-CMR	0	West Point

*Tie

Gentlemanly Game. The Lion (RMC) and the Army Mule (USMA) are depicted in the penalty box. The first penalty in this series wasn't called until the 23rd game in 1954 in Kingston when a West Point cadet was sent to the box.

PENALTY BOX

RMC VS WESTPOINT!

– HART –

"Who Can Stop Old RMC? West Point, that's who! Cartoonist Hart had fun showing the triumph of the American eagle over the RMC arm.

CHAPTER FIVE

The Depressing Thirties

The 1930s brought economic depression and a downturn in Kingston's winning of provincial championships.

Minor or youth hockey, including "a welfare league," came into its own with organized groups for several ages. And the Kingston City League, headed by dedicated sportsmen like Arthur Casterton, Melville (Star) Reid, Charlie Reynolds and Karl Leishman administered 13 teams—including Napanee, Gananoque and Brockville — playing in spirited competition at the Jock Harty rink.

And local fans, who knew the professionals only through radio and newspapers, saw the big-league game for the first time as NHL teams discovered Kingston as a training base. This combination helped produce several talented players who took the city name throughout North America.

1931 YOUTH HOCKEY GROWS

Only junior and juvenile leagues were available to youths until late in the 1920s. After the stock market crashed, divisions were set up for

Royal Military College, OHA Intermediate Champions, 1931. Coached by the legendary Tom Gelley, RMC won Kingston's first hockey championship of the 1930s.

Top row: L.C. Goodeve, K.M. Holloway, Thomas Gelley, R. Richmond; Second row: G.J. Bigelow, S. Blanchard, W.P. Carr, W.H.P. Elkins, R.G. Storms, R.W. Armstrong, K.G. Francis; Third row: F.E. White, J.N. Lane, A.J. Kennedy; Bottom row: H.K. Peck, J.S. Irvin, J.G. Carr, J.L. McAvity.

midgets and bantams, and there was a separate group for "welfare boys." The Kiwanis and Rotary clubs and Spalding sporting goods were prominent in their sponsorships, while men like E.R. Richards, Star Reid and Roy (Dutch) Dougall were prominent in organizing and officiating games at "the Jock" for the Jack Elder Trophy and other cups. Some of the teams were treated to out-of-town exhibitions as far away as Belleville.

Kingston fans were thrilled by the performance of local boy George Patterson. Packing 180 pounds on a six-foot frame, he was attracting attention for his shifty style and "uncanny way of breaking up plays." The Joyceville native broke in with Toronto and Montreal Canadiens before hitting his stride this season with the New York Americans.

The gentlemen cadets of RMC gave Kingston its only honour by winning the intercollegiate championship.

1932

THE LEAFS TRAIN IN KINGSTON

The "world champion" Toronto Maple Leafs of the NHL checked into the Hotel LaSalle for training at the Harty arena, including tennis game conditioning on Queen's University courts. In the first professional game ever played in Kingston, the Stanley Cup-holders defeated Syracuse Chiefs of the International League 5-3 in a charity game before 2,000 spectators. The Leafs, coached by Dick Irvin and managed by Conny Smythe, were "a revelation of speed and clever stickhandling," it was reported.

1933

THE HABS WERE HERE!

The Montreal Candiens, led by "The Mighty Atom" —Aurel Joliat—and dazzling speedster Howie Morenz, came to town for training in November. The Habs were "a wonder," but Kingston fans had all eyes on two members of the Stanley Cup-winning New York Rangers in the first all-NHL exhibition played here.

Bill and Bun Cook, who first played shinny on Keating's Pasture in Kingston, took time out to referee a Belleville-Hemlock Dairy City League game while coach Lester Patrick watched. The Rangers won 3-0 before 3,000 who paid $1 for a reserved seat and 35 cents for "rush." Canadiens manager Newsy Lalonde, 46, was given "a wonderful birthday party" by host Allan Randolph of the LaSalle Hotel and visited the gravesite of hockey great Marty Walsh, who had died of consumption in 1915 aged 31.

The Kiwanis Square bantam league was going great guns with teams supported by Cities Service and Doc Myles, Baker's Dairy and Doyle's Bakery. Kenny Partis won the most valuable player cup, and the late Ray Baker was remembered for his contri-

Stanley Cup Champion Toronto Maple Leafs. The Leafs held their training camp in Kingston in 1932, playing tennis in full uniform on the leaf-dotted courts of Queen's University and doing their callisthenics—push-ups on a gravel roadway! The next year the Montreal Canadiens trained at the Jock Harty Arena and met the New York Rangers and the Cook brothers in an exhibition game.

Three Cook Brothers, 1932-33. Bill, Alex (Bud) and Bun Cook met during an exhibition game as the New York Rangers played Bud's Boston Cubs of the International-American League.

Cup Winning Goal, 1933. New York Rangers Captain Bill Cook received the Stanley Cup from NHL President Frank Calder, as veteran players (right to left) Bun Cook, Frank Boucher, Ching Johnson, Andy Aitkenhead and Earl Seibert smile approvingly. Bill scored the Cup winning goal to beat the defending champion Toronto Maple Leafs.

bution to the small boys league. The next season, it was declared, all of this year's roster would be eligible and any newcomers "under 115 pounds." Two 30-minute games were played each Monday and Friday between 4 and 5 p.m.

Elsewhere in 1933, an eye injury ended the NHL career of Kingston goaltender James (Flat) Walsh. In seven NHL seasons with the Montreal Maroons and the New York Americans Walsh posted a 2.31 goals against average.

1934 BIRTH OF GRAPES

Icemakers at the Jock Harty Arena, including the legendary Alfie Pierce, had to paint a four-inch wide blue line on the ice for the first time. The two-inch wide lines were hard to see in the heavy going in this era before the introduction of resurfacing of the ice between periods.

Unheralded on February 5 was the birth of Donald Stewart Cherry, son of Del and Maude Cherry, who would grew up in the shadow of the Kingston fairgrounds and the future Memorial Centre.

1935 KINGSTONIAN COACHES WEST POINT

One of the first victims of the Depression was women's hockey. Queen's folded its team.

On the other college campus, RMC cadets were surprised when West Point, coached by ex-Kingstonian Ray Marchand, came from behind a 3-0 deficit to force a 4-4 tie in the annual international match.

Elsewhere, a future Kingston resident, Gus Marker, helped Montreal Maroons win the Stanley Cup. His reward for winning hockey's most prestigious prize: "A pocket watch and a train ticket home." The following year Marker played in the longest game in NHL history—six periods of overtime—before losing a play-off to Detroit.

1936 HANK AND JOHNNY AND KEN

Doc Myles' Dunlop Fort team won the Kingston and District league and captured the invitational juvenile tournament by defeating Upper Canada College's Junior B team at Maple Leaf Gardens. Captain John Carr-Harris at right wing and centre-man Ken (Artso) Partis led the team to a 5-3 victory and were treated to the Chicago-Toronto game on Saturday night.

Kingston juniors, most of them of juvenile age, won 13 of 16 games with Henry (Hank) Goldup, a gangling left winger, scoring 29 goals to Catlin's 28 and Partis's 24. Five of Goldup's goals came in a 10-4 win over Queen's. Queen's continued its policy of hiring former Kingston professionals to coach the

Yip Radley and Lionel Conacher. Future Kingston citizen Harry 'Yip' Radley (left) had the privilege of playing defence for the 1937 Montreal Maroons alongside Hall of Famer Lionel Conacher. Radley finished his hockey career in Kingston in 1942 with the OHA Intermediate Champion Combines.

National Bakeries, Kiwanis Bantam Champions, 1934. At least three of these players graduated to higher-level championship teams.
Front row: Len Crawford, R.G. Cook; Second row: A. Johnson, K.G. Martin, John Carr-Harris, J.H. Simpson, Ken Partis, D. McDougall,
B. Robertson; Back row: W.H. Martin G. Quirt, M. Heagle, J.L. Forest, D. Lewers, J. McCormack, J.J. (Star) Reid, H.M. Wilder.

Hemlock Dairy, 1933-34. This local team rated individual photographs while playing in the Kingston City League. Coach Senator Powell had a strong contingent that included Tom Thurlby (upper left) and William (Bump) Watts, a future icemaker (lower right).

senior intercollegiate team. James (Flat) Walsh, a solid goaltender with the Montreal Maroons and New York Americans from 1927 to 1933, directed the Tricolour, which competed for the first time in an international intercollegiate league and promptly whipped New Jersey's Princeton Tigers 6-1.

1937 ROTARIANS WELCOME MITES

The Rotary Mite league for boys "around 13 years" was organized at a meeting at the YMCA. Star Reid also organized a beginners league. The following season the league donated a gift to the league's leading scorer, Jack Dickson.

Elswhere in 1937, another future Kingston resident, Sylvanus Apps, broke in with the Toronto Maple Leafs and won the Calder Trophy as the NHL's Rookie of the Year.

1938 RED INDIANS TRIUMPH

The development of minor hockey paid off this year in the OHA Junior B division when Kingston Red Indians, coached and sponsored by Wally Elmer, won 15 of 17 league and playoff games and the Ontario championship. The Red Indians easily topped Whitby, won a four-team round-robin series and ousted Barrie Colts in three consecutive games—4-0, 6-4 and 10-5. Nick Knott, Johnnie Carr-Harris, Jerry Younger-Lewis, Aimer Burtch and Ken Partis shone on the attack, while Bob

Nesbitt, Don Crawford and Mack Rochefort were defensive stalwarts.

Bun Cook, after a 10-year career with the New York Rangers and the Boston Bruins, began a successful coaching career in the American Hockey League. Cook's teams in Providence and Cleveland would win seven Calder Cup championships.

1939 A HOLLYWOOD FINISH

Royal Military College, after winning 11 consecutive annual matches against West Point, fell to the Americans 3-2. The USMA, following the tradition of RMC in donating a trophy to the losing side, presented one to the Canadians, "to commemorate their unique sports rivalry." Ironically, the whole ice action at the Jock Harty Arena was captured on film for a Hollywood movie starring Robert Taylor.

1940 SERVICE CLUBS AID YOUTH

In the 10th year of the decade, and with the Second World War raging, RMC cadets packed up their hockey gear and donned different uniforms. The Kiwanis, Lions and Rotary service clubs organized four minor hockey groups. Chairman was W.J. (Bill) Watts with Star Reid as supervisor. Max Jackson, who represented Kingston and area on the Ontario Minor Hockey Association, handled the league publicity.

Kingston Dunlop Forts, Juvenile Champs, 1936. Doc Myles was one of the big supporters of boy's hockey in the 1930s and 1940s. His Dunlop Forts won the Spalding invitational Juvenile series at Toronto in 1936. Front row: William McNaul, Don Wilkinson, Aimer Burtch, William Lafferty, Len Crawford, Bill Lemmon; Back row: Doc Myles, Art McGlashan, Jack Manson, Ken Partis, Jack Crawford, Gord Clark, John Carr-Harris, Don Crawford, Gerald Lewis, Carl Hewitt, Jack Scott, E.R. Richards, Lewis Grooms.

Bill Taugher, 1936. Former Kingston junior Bill Taugher starred for six years with Buffalo Bisons of the AHL. His puck-stopping gyrations caught the attention of a Cleveland Plain-Dealer cartoonist, who cited Canada and Kingston as "the incubator of great hockey players."

Henry (Hank) Goldup, 1940. When Hank Goldup left Kingston in 1937, he never looked back, playing the next season as a Toronto Marlboro and leading the Major Junior A League in scoring with 25 goals and 41 points in 14 games. He played six-seasons in the NHL with the Leafs and Rangers, winning a Stanley Cup in Toronto in 1942.

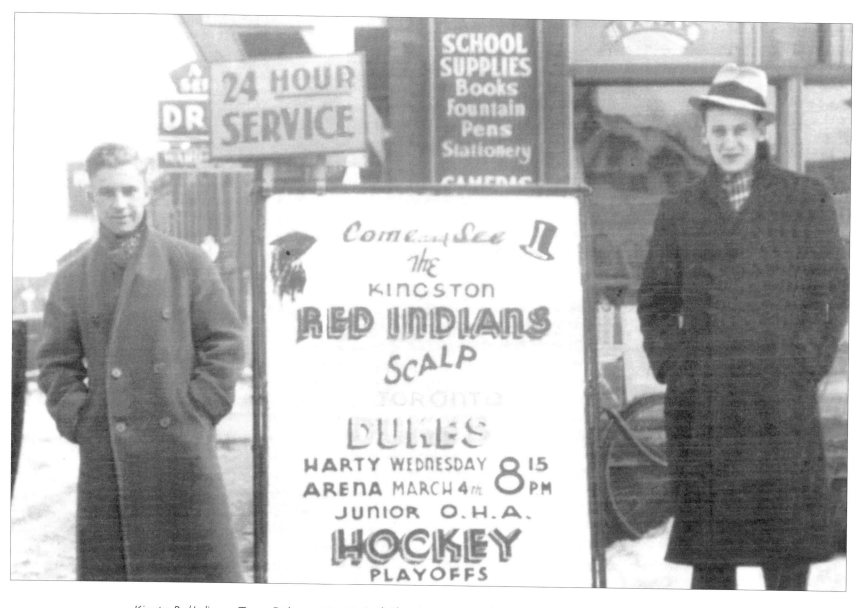

Kingston Red Indians vs Toronto Dukes, 1936. Joey Catlin (left) and Hank Goldup (right), both members of the Kingston Junior B Red Indians and future professionals, pose alongside a sign promoting a playoff game. The Kingston team was sponsored by Wally Elmer's service station that sold Red Indian (Texaco) gasoline.

OSCAR SIMPSON
TRAINER

WALLY ELMER
COACH

CARL LEISHMAN
PRESIDENT

AB. STINSON
VICE PRES.

STAN. HALL
SEC. TREAS.

KINGSTON
RED INDIANS
O.H.A. JUNIOR B CHAMPIONS
1938

PLAYED
17 GAMES
WON 15
LOST 2

DEFEATED
BARRIE
FINAL SERIES
4-0, 6-4, 10-5

MACK. ROCHEFORT
DEFENCE

CARL HEWITT
GOAL

BOB NESBITT
S. DEFENCE

MELL. ESFORD
L. WING

O.H.A. JUNIOR B TROPHY

JIMMIE SIMPSON
GOAL

AIMER BURTCH
CENTRE

JOHNNIE CARR-HARRIS
R. WING

DOUG. JESSE
S. DEFENCE

SONNY CORRIGAN
MASCOT

BUD GOODFELLOW
DEFENCE

LENNY CRAWFORD
R. WING

NICK KNOTT
L. WING

JERRY YOUNGER-LEWIS
L. WING

MACK JACKSON
MANAGER

KEN PARTIS
CENTRE

DON. CRAWFORD
DEFENCE

Kingston Red Indians, Ontario Junior B Champions, 1938. One of the finest teams ever to represent Kingston, the Red Indians won 15 of 17 games to capture the Ontario title, Kingston's 13th provincial championship in 25 finals. From the top row down: Oscar Simpson, Wally Elmer (Coach), Carl Leishman, Ab Stinson, Stan Hall; Carl Hewitt, Mack Rochefort; Bob Nesbitt, Mel Esford, Jimmie Simpson, Aimer Burtch; Johnny Carr-Harris, Doug Jesse, Sunny Corrigian (Mascot), Bud Goodfellow; Len Crawford; Nick Knot, Jerry Younger-Lewis, Max Jackson (Manager), Ken Partis, Don Crawford.

Canada's First Hockey Hall *of* Fame

The International Hockey Hall of Fame and Museum

IT ALL STARTED WITH A BALL . . . .

The International Hockey Hall of Fame and Museum owes its beginning to one man—James Thomas Sutherland—who played in the first league games in Kingston in the 1890s. The Kingston native refereed, coached and managed championship teams and held hockey's highest administrative offices. An itinerant shoe salesman, he spread the word about Kingston's hockey heritage throughout North America.

He conceived the idea of a shrine to honour the greats of the game in 1939 —shortly before the outbreak of the Second World War. In his quest, Capt. Sutherland, who attained his army rank during the First World War, was inspired by a ball, not a puck. The National Baseball Hall of Fame had opened in Cooperstown, New York in June, 1939. As past president of the Ontario Hockey Association and the Canadian Amateur Hockey Association, "Cap'n Jim's" enthusiasm for the project and his popularity among hockey moguls moved the CAHA in 1941 to appoint a three-man committee to investigate the origin of hockey in Canada. As this debate raged, Sutherland landed the Hall of Fame in Kingston.

"Hockey needs such a shrine," said a Montreal writer, "because that is the only way the hardy pioneers of hockey can be given the honour that is their due."

That idea, although periodically mentioned in the press, was not officially recognized until one year later in April 1943, when the City of Kingston invited the CAHA to establish a hall of fame along the lines of the baseball shrine in Cooperstown, New York. Canada's amateur hockey officials referred the final decision to the National Hockey League, and in September of that year, both bodies sanctioned Kingston as *the most central site* to erect a Hall of Fame "as a memorial dedicated to perpetuate the memories of men who have done so much to develop nationally and internationally, Canada's great winter sport—hockey."

"That innocuous-looking phrase, *'the most central site'* covers one of the stiffest inter-city arguments to rage around the origin of hockey since the game was invented," said *Montreal* Gazette columnist Dink Carroll. Montreal was in the thick of the debate. Countered Capt. Sutherland: "The Hall will be built in Kingston regardless of where the first puck was shot."

Kingstonians, led by the indomitable. Sutherland and supported by City Hall stalwarts stood strong and won out over multiple protests. Sutherland, then 73, was delighted, and while Kingston's mayor and a city councillors headed up key committees, the venerable creator of the Hall of Fame dream was named a member of every committee.

With great enthusiasm the local committee proceeded with plans to raise funds for an appropriate building. A goal of $20,000 was set but rising costs in the post-war period soon hiked that to $50,000. The City of Kingston gave $5,000 to the building fund. The CAHA donated $10,000. The NHL contributed $7,500 and later pledged $30,000 ($5,000 from each of the six teams), but that promise was never kept.

In three-years, the fund-raising, boosted by exhibition games involving the Boston Bruins, New York Rangers, Chicago Black Hawks, Toronto Maple Leafs, Montreal Canadiens, and the amateur Hamilton Tigers and Toronto Marlboros and Montreal Royals, topped $45,000, but the NHL hiked the ante. The NHL ruled $150,000 as inadequate for a building project and in 1954 set a new goal of $250,000.

Frontenac County Courthouse grounds, the former Cooke's United Church, and Old Fort Henry were suggested and rejected as sites for the shrine.

One year later a Sports Hall of Fame was established at Toronto's Canadian National Exhibition grounds. It included a "National Hockey Hall of Fame" with 23 players and 10 builders— all of whom had been elected to the International Hockey Hall of Fame in Kingston. In September 1955, 12 years after the joyous news of Kingston's selection as the Hall site was announced, Capt. Sutherland died. He was 85 and never saw the local shrine arise. The Kingston hall, modelled after the Cooperstown shrine, was built on the Kingston Memorial Centre grounds in 1961 and formally opened in 1965.

By 1958, when President Clarence Campbell announced that the NHL had transferred its allegiance to Toronto, 42 players and builders had been "inducted" into the homeless Kingston shrine. "The Kingston Forty-Two"—saluted in a 1973 brochure —represent some of the greatest players and builders of the sport. Here are their names and the years of their "induction" into the original Hall in Kingston:

Capt. James T. Sutherland and Clarence Campbell, 1947. Every "Original Six" team played an exhibition in Kingston at Jock Harty Arena to raise funds for building a hockey hall of fame, but the proceeds were never sufficient to start construction. Hall of Fame founder Capt. James T. Sutherland and NHL President Clarence Campbell were front and centre for the opening exhibition game: New York Rangers vs. Hamilton Tigers.

Hall of Fame. This preliminary sketch by Drever and Smith of Kingston for the International Hockey Hall of Fame was based on the design of the Baseball of Hall of Fame, opened in Cooperstown, New York, 1939.

THE KINGSTON FORTY-TWO

1945:   Howie Morenz, George Vezina, Hobey Baker, Harvey Pulford, Eddie Gerard, Frank McGee, Hod Stuart, Charlie Gardiner, Tom Phillips, Lord Stanley and Sir Montagu Allan.

1947:   Dit Clapper, Cyclone Taylor, Eddie Shore, Frank Nighbor, Aurel Joliat, Russell Bowie, Lester Patrick, John Ross Robertson, Art Ross, Francis Nelson, William Hewitt, William Northey, Frank Calder, Claude C. Robinson and Capt. James T. Sutherland.

1949:   Russell Bain.

1950:   Newsy Lalonde, Joe Malone, Frank Patrick, Scotty Davidson, Charles Drinkwater, Mike Grant, Si Griffis, Harry Trihey and George Richardson.

1952:   Dickie Boon, Bill Cook, Moose Goheen, Moose Johnson, Mickie MacKay and Nels Stewart.

After the NHL stepped in, the IHHF continued to honour the same new members inducted in Toronto, with two exceptions. In 1966, the Kingston Hall inducted Fred J. (Bun) Cook of Kingston and Harvey (Busher) Jackson of Toronto. Both were later installed in the players' section of the Toronto Hall.

In the first 12 years of operation, the Hall was under the direction of the Kingston Community Memorial Centre and exhibits were confined to the second storey. The first floor was a public hall, used for dances, stag parties, wedding receptions, a distinct contrast to the conception of a shrine to honour the greats of Canada's winter sport.

In 1978, the IHHF Board of Directors, with City Council approval, took over the complete building and raised $25,000 for renovations and a complete redesign. At the re-opening, two hockey VIPS, Frank J. Selke and Clarence S. Campbell, who had worked tirelessly to establish the Hall in Kingston and later to move it to Toronto, were among the speakers. The president of the NHL, then 73, the same age when Capt. Sutherland clinched the shrine for Kingston, said, with a tear in his eye: "Capt. James T. Sutherland conceived the idea of an international hockey hall of fame. . .to be erected in a place he believed as the real point of origin of hockey." The NHL president congratulated "all who have had the courage and tenacity to maintain faith in his dream" and for their determination to improve the shrine.

The Hall took on a true worldly outlook when a municipal Task Force recommendation resulted in a three-way agreement with the International Ice Hockey Federation, the City of Kingston, and the IHHFM board of directors. The move, accomplished with a $100,000 line of credit from the City, resulted in an influx of international exhibits, but the Switzerland-based body never took advantage of the opportunity and the agreement died an unnatural death after the passing of IIHF President Gunther Sabetzki.

In the past quarter century, the Hall of Fame and Museum has welcomed hundreds of hockey buffs from nearly every state in America and from countries extending from Australia and Japan to Hawaii, England, Finland and Sweden. It has played hosts to hockey legends Gordie Howe and Bobby Hull, Maurice and Henri Richard, and has exhibited the Stanley Cup and the Allan Cup.

In the late 1990s, the Kingston directors, headed by Roy B. Conacher, initiated a holding pattern while awaiting efforts to relocate the museum in the downtown tourist trail. Despite many studies and proposals, and a switch in name from "Hall of Fame" to "Museum," the shrine entered into the new millennium in its original location in the Kingston fairgrounds.

In 2000, under the aggressive leadership of new president Mark Potter, the museum took on an "Original Six" appearance, downplayed world hockey, and gave more exposure to Kingston men and women players. To improve marketing possibilities, a new 60th anniversary logo was introduced along with the original name—The International Hockey Hall of Fame and Museum, Inc.—and a website created.

Open daily, Monday to Saturday and Sunday afternoons from June to September and on Saturday afternoons and by appointment for groups during the off-season, "the little shrine that wouldn't quit" plays hosts to the true hockey aficionado. The visitor's log sparkles with accolades of visitors, young and old: "Great," "Fantastic," Wonderful", "Terrific," "Cool," "Awesome," "Absolutely outstanding," and "Great history brought back to life."

The Hall has had a rough but resilient career under the direction of volunteers and a few part-time summer employees—one that might have pleased and perplexed founder Sutherland.

Roll of Honour for The Silver Fox (top). Lester Patrick, coach and manager of the early New York Rangers, displays a copy of the page from The Roll of Honour outlining his storied career, with Capt. Sutherland, Gen. Kilpatrick (the head of Madison Square Gardens) and Kingston Mayor Stuart Crawford attending.

Stanley Cup Celebration, 1970 (bottom). Hundreds of Kingston hockey fans turned out to the International Hockey Hall of Fame to honour Rick Smith and Wayne Cashman of the Stanley Cup champion Boston Bruins. The honoured guests also included Danny McLeod and broadcaster Ted Darling.

Bobby Hull Exhibit. The Golden Jet officially unveiled his collection at the International Hockey Hall of Fame in 1990.

Historic Hockey Series. Queen's and RMC square off in the annual re-enactment of the first game played on the Kingston harbour in 1886.

Roll of Honour

Captain James T. Sutherland

One of the
Veterans of Canadian Hockey
and Founder of

The International Hockey Hall of Fame

Were there one pedestal in the International Hockey Hall of Fame to be occupied by one person who pioneered Hockey and then gave a lifetime of devotion and work to the Sport, that person would be

Captain James T. Sutherland

Born in Kingston, Ontario, October 10th 1870, Jim Sutherland played hockey in the first organized league of which there is record. The teams consisted of Queen's University, the Royal Military College, the Kingstons and the Athletics. He played "Point," a defense position, on the last named Club. Queen's won the championship, defeating the Athletics 3-0 in the final game.

Later, Captain Sutherland organized the Frontenacs, which, under his management won numerous Junior and intermediate titles in the Ontario Hockey Championship series. He became President of the Ontario Hockey Association and of the Canadian Amateur Hockey Association, and has been elected a life member of both. During World War One, he served four years with the Canadian Forces Overseas.

Captain James T. Sutherland well may be called the "Father of Hockey". He has devoted 64 years to the betterment of the Sport, and it is quite understandable that in recent years he has devoted his complete time to the Hockey Hall of Fame, which through his efforts was located in his native Kingston, Ontario, where it will be a lasting Memorial to this grand Sportsman and Gentleman.

Contributed by
Arthur H. Ross
Vice-President and Manager
Boston Bruins N.H.L. Hockey Club
Boston, Mass, U.S.A.

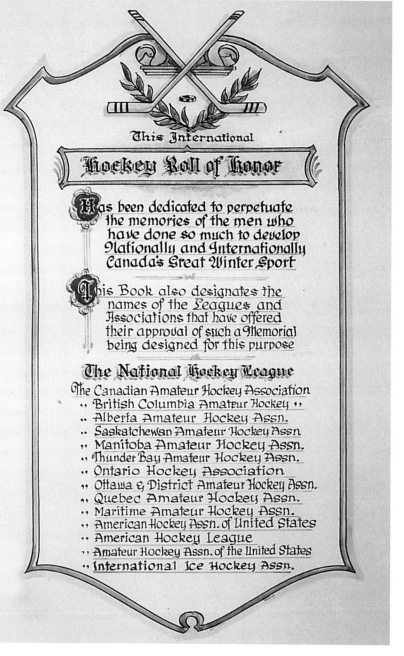

This International
Hockey Roll of Honor

Has been dedicated to perpetuate the memories of the men who have done so much to develop Nationally and Internationally Canada's Great Winter Sport

This Book also designates the names of the Leagues and Associations that have offered their approval of such a Memorial being designed for this purpose

The National Hockey League

The Canadian Amateur Hockey Association
" British Columbia Amateur Hockey "
" Alberta Amateur Hockey Assn.
" Saskatchewan Amateur Hockey Assn.
" Manitoba Amateur Hockey Assn.
" Thunder Bay Amateur Hockey Assn.
" Ontario Hockey Association
" Ottawa & District Amateur Hockey Assn.
" Quebec Amateur Hockey Assn.
" Maritime Amateur Hockey Assn.
" American Hockey Assn. of United States
" American Hockey League
" Amateur Hockey Assn. of the United States
" International Ice Hockey Assn.

Hockey Roll of Honour. Designed by George Wakeling, the "Hockey Roll of Honour" records the International Hockey Hall of Fame's heritage.

Bread Line. New York Rangers "Bread Line" featured Bill and 'Bun' Cook of Kingston with Frank Boucher, the NHL's highest scoring line in the 1920s and early 1930s, who helped the Rangers win two Stanley Cups.

Hockey's Oldest Jersey. Queen's University jersey from 1895 worn by captain Guy Curtis.

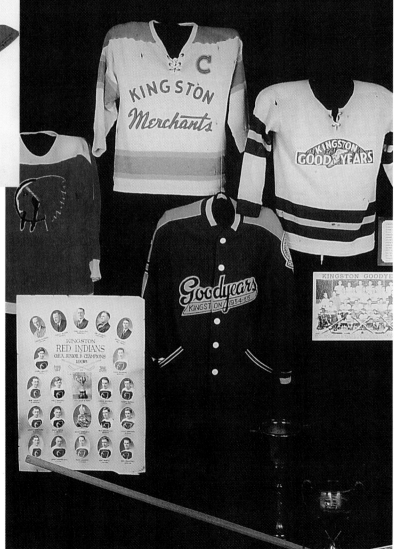

*Kingston Team Sweaters (right and next page). The nickname 'Frontenacs' has graced
Kingston hockey jersey's for over 100 years, but the 'Aces', 'Canadians', 'Goodyears',
'Red Indians', 'CKLCs' and 'Merchants' are well remembered.*

Kingston Frontenacs, EPHL Champions, 1962-63. Front row: Bob Goy, Wayne Connelly, Pat Stapleton, Jim Magee (Pres), Wren Blair (Coach/GM), Harry Sinden (Asst Coach), Don Blackburn, Bruce Gamble; Second row: Bun Cook, Gerry Ouelette, Pete Panagabko, Jean-Paul Parisee, Ron Willey, Randy Miller, Alf Treen, Tom Dickinson; Back row: Dick Cherry, Jeannot Gilbert, Wayne Schultz, Billy Knibbs, Cliff Pennington Ken Stephenson, Howie Dietrich.

Wallace R. Berry

Kingston Gurnsey Realtors, Wrigley Cup Finalists, 1973-74. Front row: Kim Elliott, Brian Clancy, Rob Plumb, Rick Laporte, Gord Botting, Rick Coupland, Ken Linseman, Bruce Munroe, Bill Jenkins; Back row: Randy Skeggs (Trainer), David Little, Mike Gilpin, Cam MacGregor, Tim Torrance, Mike Simurda, Gerry Wagar (Coach), Harvey Milne, Garry Sherbert, Peter Young, Jim Hare (Manager).

Twice a Stanley Cup champion, Wayne Cashman played his entire 17-year NHL career with the Boston Bruins.

A steady stay-at-home defenceman, Rick Smith played 14-years of pro hockey and won a Stanley Cup with the Boston Bruins in 1970.

WEEKEND MAGAZINE is published
as part of these 33 newspapers:
BRANDON Daily Sun
BRANTFORD Expositor
CALGARY Albertan
CHARLOTTETOWN Patriot
CORNER BROOK, NFLD. Western Star
EDMONTON Journal
FORT WILLIAM Daily Times-Journal
HAMILTON Spectator
KINGSTON Whig-Standard
KIRKLAND LAKE Northern Daily News
LETHBRIDGE Herald
LONDON Free Press

MEDICINE HAT News
MONCTON Times and Transcript
MONTREAL Star
MOOSE JAW Times-Herald
NORTH BAY Daily Nugget
OTTAWA Citizen
PETERBOROUGH Examiner
PORT ARTHUR News-Chronicle
PRINCE ALBERT Daily Herald
QUEBEC Chronicle-Telegraph
RED DEER Advocate
SAINT JOHN Telegraph-Journal and
    Evening Times-Globe
ST. JOHN'S, NFLD. Evening Telegram
SUDBURY Star

SYDNEY Cape Breton Post
TIMMINS Daily Press
TORONTO Telegram
VANCOUVER Sun
VICTORIA Sunday Times
WINNIPEG Tribune
THE STANDARD
PERSPECTIVES is published
as part of these six newspapers:
GRANBY La Voix de l'Est
MONTRÉAL Le Dimanche-Matin
OTTAWA Le Droit
QUÉBEC Le Soleil
SHERBROOKE La Tribune
TROIS-RIVIÈRES Le Nouvelliste

Weekend
MAGAZINE

Vol. 12, No. 8   Feb. 24, 1962

Gambling:
Big Crime
Lives On
Small Bets
Page 8

KEN'S A BORN HOCKEY PLAYER — SEE PAGE 23

George Lilley

Featured on the cover of this 1962 edition of Weekend Magazine, *Ken Linseman was tabbed as a future star at the age of three.*

Edmonton Oilers Ken Linseman battles Philadelphia Flyers star Bobby Clarke. Linseman scored the Stanley Cup winning goal for Edmonton as the Oilers won their first NHL championship in 1984.

Kirk Muller's finest moment in a 19-year NHL career came in 1993 when he scored the Stanley Cup winning goal for Montreal against the L.A. Kings.

Doug Gilmour is one of the most popular players in Toronto Maple Leafs history and holds their single season scoring record with 127 points in the 1992-93 season.

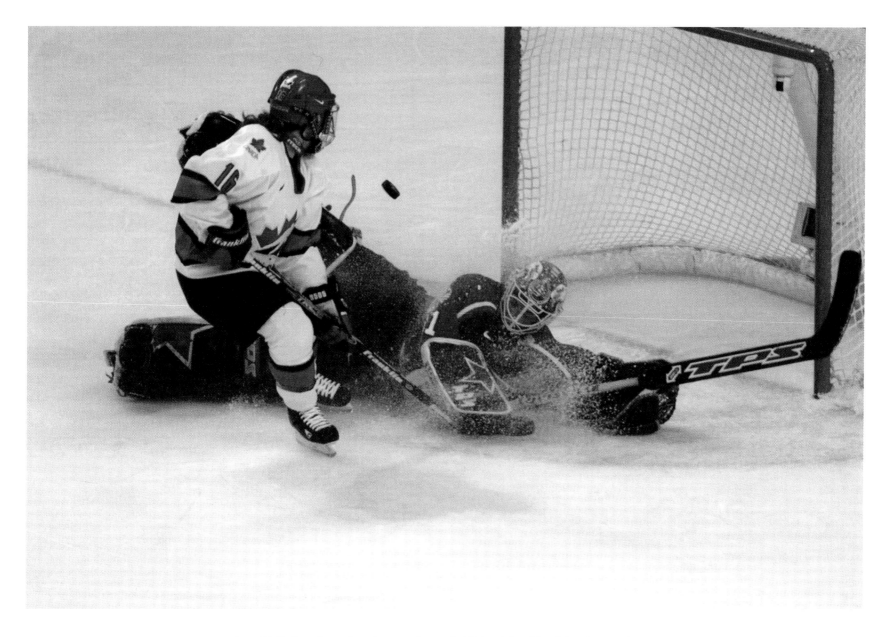

Jayna Hefford's goal gave Canada a 3-2 win over the USA and the gold medal at the 2002 Olympics.

Don Cherry. Hockey Night in Canada's "Coach's Corner."

Mr. Hockey. Despite an arthritic wrist, Gordie Howe spent hours signing hundreds of autographs for Kingston kids during Gordie Howe Day at the International Hockey Hall of Fame in 1972.

CHAPTER SIX

The Fighting Forties

The 1940s were a time of drastic change, with young Kingston players switching to khaki and blue uniforms and other armed service men coming to this garrison city to learn soldiering—and to play hockey. It was an age of service hockey with officers recruiting the top professionals for the glory of their regiments or training base. Kingston was no exception.

The Hall of Fame movement, inspired by baseball's Cooperstown shrine, caught on here, and Kingston, after a concentrated campaign, was selected as the most central site for a new shrine. There was the most significant change in the game with the addition of a new line on the ice—one that sped up the game and helped extend the playing careers of many men regarded as too old for active service life.

1941 CITY COMBINES FOR A CROWN

Despite the loss of players to the navy, army and air force, the city, Queen's and RMC combined to mould a championship team in the OHA Senior B series. The Kingston Combines had a good mixture of

Kingston Collegiate Institute Hockey Team, 1944. Front row: Ron Shaw, Greg Weese, Tom Boutillier, Don Keenleyside, Charles (Flicker) Flint; Back row: Coach Stan Stewart, Art Berry, Carl Hartman, Pete Webber, Bob Bailey, Bill Campbell, Bob Joyce, Floyd Holland.

Regiopolis College Hockey Team. Players boys pose in a variety of sweaters. Bill Gourdier, lower right, tried to fill out the jersey of the Army Frontenacs, Kingston's star studded Second World War senior team.

youth and experience and rolled to victory over Belleville, Peterborough, Whitby, Trenton RCAF and Hamilton to qualify for the final. Reinstated professional Harry (Yip) Radley and Clair Williamson were stalwarts on defence, but Bob and Jim Neilson and Mel Williamson supplied the scoring talent. In the best-of-seven final against Tommy Burlington's Owen Sound Greys, Williamson, a tricky centreman, topped all point-getters with seven goals and 12 assists as the Kingston Combines won four games to one.

It was the first season of the new face-off circle—a 10-foot radius —designed to help the referee keep wingers from interfering with the facing centremen. Previous to this innovation, only a large dot marked the spot where the puck was dropped.

Capt. Sutherland, who had extolled Kingston as the birthplace of hockey, was appointed to a three-man Canadian Amateur Hockey Association committee to study the origin of the game. One year later, he was rewarded when Kingston was selected as the most central site to erect a hall of fame "as a memorial to . . . Canada's great winter sport—hockey." *Whig-Standard* sport editor Mike Rodden wrote prophetically: "The population of Kingston has never grasped the significance of this award."

1942

THE FIRST OMHA CROWN

Kingston's minor hockey program produced its first provincial championship, thanks to the coaching, leadership and support of William (Squeak) Reason, future mayor William Mills and sponsor James de St. Remy. The Saints won the Ontario Minor Hockey Association Midget crown behind the playing of such future stars as Ed Plumb, Bud Aitken, Ted Fowler and Fred Gurnsey, all of whom would play a part in Kingston's future hockey program.

Capt. Sutherland, in a radio broadcast over the new station CKWS, extolled the current Kingston Frontenacs, with Gus Giesbrecht, Hub Macey, Mel Williamson, Joey Catlin, Mickey Blake and Johnny Carr-Harris named as the most outstanding team in the city's history. It was high praise as the 72-year-old hockey veteran recounted 31 major honours, including 15 Senior, six Intermediate and eight provincial Junior championships, plus an Allan Cup victory and three Stanley Cup challenges.

1943

A LINE AT CENTRE ICE

With many of the top professional stars serving in the armed forces and the game slowed by "ganging attacks," the CAHA and the NHL decided to speed

Kingston Army Frontenacs, 1944. This team was touted as Allan Cup contenders before the Canadian military put an end to service teams playing for Ontario and Canadian honours. Front row: Alvin (Buck) Jones, Jim Peters, Jack Tisdale, Doug Stevenson, Ken Booth, Lloyd (Red) Doran, Charlie Phillips; Second row: Major Tanner, Chuck Corrigan Vic Grigg, George (Red) Hamill, Roy (Gus) Giesbrecht, Len (Moe) White, Jack MacDonald, Major Ed Watts; Third row: James T. Sutherland, William Walshe, Lorne Cook, James de St. Remy, W.J. Watts, Wally Elmer, Jack Trenhailer; Insets: Bill Mortimer, Herb Mortimer, Jim Galbraith, Bill Dodd.

up the action. Introduced was a red line at centre ice, which permitted passing out of the defensive zone over the blue line to the half-way point.

Local players making up the wartime league of Garrison, Ordnance, Navy and Queen's teams competing for the Van Horne Trophy also had to adapt to a new face-off rule. The centremen were required to face the end of the rink instead of the sides, as had been done since hockey first copied the lacrosse style face.

Kingston fans missed some of their old hometown favourites, but the incoming players more than made up for the loss. The Army Frontenacs, led by playing coach Red Hamill, attracted more than 13,000 paid admissions to the Harty Arena for OHA Senior and exhibition games. The biggest attractions were the Boston Bruins and the Montreal Canadiens, but Hamilton, Toronto, St. Catharines and Cornwall service and civilian teams also drew well. Hamill, a former Chicago Black Hawk, was second in league scoring, but three other former NHLers, Roy Giesbrecht, Red Doran and Jim Peters, played prominent roles in Kingston's one year of hosting soldier skaters. Giesbrecht, playing for Kingston in the Ottawa Senior Hockey League, scored three goals in 79 seconds.

The wartime news, marred by casualty reports, brought further sadness with the report that William Taugher, after a long career as a goaltender in the minor pro leagues, had died.

1944

A MOST VALUABLE PLAYER

Kingston Frontenacs-Army, with 12 ex-professionals in the line-up, defeated Toronto Navy, 13-9, in aid of the Hall of Fame building fund. The club, entered in the OHA Senior league, was disbanded after they losing 11-3 to Detroit Red Wings in an exhibition game at Jock Harty Arena. Ottawa decreed that armed forces' teams would no longer be permitted to compete for the Allan Cup. Army, navy and air force officials at several bases were accused of packing teams with former NHL players and not concentrating on training men for combat duties.

One of Kingston Frontenac Army's most popular players, Regina's Albert (Red) Tilson, who loved to play hockey, heeded the call and died in battle one year later in Holland. His name still lives on the OHA's most valuable player trophy.

1946

LOCOS STEAM TO VICTORY

Kingston celebrated the first season of war-free hockey with its 13th OHA Senior championship. Sponsored by the Canadian Locomotive Company, a busy waterfront industry, and coached by Dingo

Kingston Saints, Eastern Ontario Junior B Champs, 1946. Bill Reason's championship team included future NHLer Lorne Ferguson.
Front row: Bill Shepherd, Lorne Ferguson, Ron Plumb, Jim Brown, Tom Boutilier, Bob Joyce, Chuck Flint, Sam Mulholland, captain;
Second row: Ed Fuller, Al Rogers, George Graves, Doug Patterson, Bruce Woodman, Dick Davidson, Jack Danby; Back row: Mascot
Gabby White, Alf Plumb, Bill Mills, James de St. Remy (Sponsor), Bill Reason (Coach).

Kingston Locos, OHA Intermediate A Champs, 1946. Sponsored by the Canadian Locomotive Company Athletic Club, this well-balanced team won 21 of 28 games to capture the John Ross Robertson Trophy. Sitting in front, Cliff Aitken; First row: Joe Aitken, Ken Murphy Glynn Udall, Jack Stone, Ken Partis, Ken McNaughton; Second row: Joe Lay, Ted Nicholson, Harold Scrutton, John Carr-Harris, Bill Mortimer (Coach), George MacGregor, Joe Watts; Back row: Dingo Haynes, Gord Hill, Fred J. Martin, T.G. Kirby.

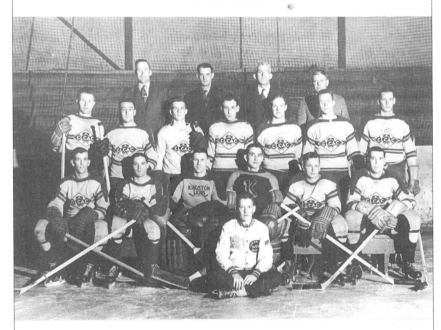

L. COOKE _{GUEST}

Canadian Locomotive Company Athletic Club

KINGSTON
ONTARIO, CANADA

Dinner

TO

1945 - 46
Intermediate "A"-O.H.A. Champions

TUESDAY, JUNE 4TH., 1946 AT 6.00 P.M.

HOTEL LA SALLE
KINGSTON

R.H. (Buddy) Aitken. Buddy Aitken returned to the Kingston Jr B Vics in
1947-48 after two seasons in Ontario's top Junior A league playing for Charlie
Conacher's Oshawa Generals and the St. Catharines Falcons. He went on to
star for Kingston Nylons and Vimy Signals before becoming a popular coach in
the Church Athletic League.

Kingston Combines, OHA Senior B Champions, 1944. Front row: Yip Radley,
Dud White, Jim Neilson, Bobby Neilson, Buck Burrows, Walt Gerow; Back
row: Pepper Martin, George Hood, Wally Elmer (Coach), Clare Williamson,
Ted Johnson, Mel Williamson, Glynn Udall, Rick Hepburn, Ray Smith.

Haynes, the "Locos" steamed to the OHA Intermediate A championship behind the attacking skills of Ken Partis, John Carr-Harris, Cliff and Joe Aitken, Joe Lay, Ted Nicholson, George MacGregor and the defensive and goaltending skills of Joe Watts and Glynn Udall, respectively. The Locos defeated Peterborough, Oshawa and Collingwood before winning the championship over Port Colborne.

Future stars were being developed by Kingston Saints, now in Junior B competition. The Reason-Mills squad won the eastern Ontario championship. Lorne Ferguson and his ability to score goals earned a tryout with Gus Marker's Tulsa Oilers. The blonde left winger potted two goals in a 4-2 victory over Toronto St. Michael Buzzers.

1947 THE NHL COMES TO KINGSTON

With the war years behind them, Kingston's young men, including several Locos, looked across the Atlantic and played a prominent role in the revival of the Scottish Ice Hockey Association. At least one, Joe Aitken, made Scotland his home and never returned.

Local fans continued to see the best players in the NHL when "the original six" played a series of exhibitions with proceeds going to the building fund of the International Hockey Hall of Fame.

Several thousand dollars were raised as Boston Bruins and New York Rangers met senior amateur clubs such as Toronto Marlboros and Hamilton Tigers, and the Chicago Black Hawks "toyed" with the Kingston-Queen's Combines, which included members of the junior Vics. Officiating most of these exhibitions was 58-year-old Mike Rodden, who had handled more than 2,000 NHL games.

Among the first inductees into the Hall of fame was Kingston's Captain Sutherland, who devoted most of his 77 years to the game and was praised for his indefatigable work to get the Hall established. While promoting the game across Canada, he still served as president of the Kingston City League.

A noted Kingston forward trio, imported by Washington Lions of the Eastern Amateur Hockey League, supplied most of the Kingston Locos' scoring power. John Carr-Harris, with 30 goals and 38 assists, was tops on the team and fourth in the four-team OHA Intermediate A league. Ken Partis (23-25-58) was eighth in the league, and line-mate Joey Catlin compiled 26 goals and 17 assists in 43 games.

In 1948, future Kingston resident Syl Apps retired from the Toronto Maple leafs after back-to-back Stanley Cup wins in 1947 and 1948.

Michael J. (Mike) Rodden. Hall of Fame referee Mike Rodden came out of retirement to work a rare pro-am exhibition game between the Hamilton Tigers and the New York Rangers at the Jock Harty Arena in support of the International Hockey Hall of Fame. As an NHL official, he refereed 1,200 games.

1950

GRAPES WAS GOOD AT 15

Another local boy who had completed a professional career returned to the ice lanes when Barriefield's Francis (Mickey) Blake took over as playing coach of the Kingston Nylons in the OHA Senior B series. The Nylons ran up victories over Belleville Diesels and Peterborough Petes but couldn't handle the Legion of the Liftlock City, the eventual Ontario champion.

A future pro caught the attention of a future hall of famer in an OHA Junior B game. Don Cherry, just a few weeks past his 16th birthday, helped set up the winning goal as Kingston Victorias defeated Peterborough Triple Links, 3-1. "The youngest player on either team looked to be the sharpest of them all," wrote *Whig-Standard* sports editor Mike Rodden in praising the underage junior for his "stellar defensive play." The performance earned Cherry a trial in the Boston farm system. Confirming Kingston's reputation as a cradle of hockey was the news that Cliff Aitken was invited to tryout with Stratford Junior A's.

The revival of women's hockey at the university level gave male scribes an opportunity to express alleged humour in headlines and story: "U of T's feminine pulchritude defeats the Golden Gals:" "The two teams—in full-hockey gear—conducted themselves in lady-like manner," noted a *Whig* male in reporting that referee Don Keenleyside called only two penalties for tripping. The most encouraging news was that the universities were considering the formation of a girl's intercollegiate hockey league.

Meanwhile, nineteen-year-old Lorne Ferguson of Kingston garnered 35 goals and 35 assists in 70 games, was nominated for Tulsa Oilers' MVP award, and earned a trial with the Boston Bruins.

Don Cherry. As a 15-year-old, Don Cherry (far right) still hadn't earned a team sweater in this team photo of the Kingston Jr. B Victorias, but his rugged play on defence earned him a sweater—and a spot in the lineup—later in the year. He went on to play for the Memorial Cup winning Barrie Flyers.

CHAPTER SEVEN

The Unforgettable Fifties

Hockey grew into long pants in the 1950s. The city, after depending on Queen's University for an artificial ice rink for 30 years, built its own arena, a living monument to the Second World War dead. The $350,000 Kingston Community Memorial Centre, located on the fairgrounds, was opened before a crowd of 3,200 fans, who watched Jack (Mucker) McKeown score the first goal on a pass from Bob Joyce as Kingston Nylons defeated Belleville Redmen 12-4. With the new facility came championships and eventually professional teams and the largest crowds in the city's history. But with the crowning glory in provincial hockey and healthy gate splits came the most embarrassing happening in the history of the game, an event that still makes some Kingstonians squirm or clam up.

1951

BLACK MARK ON THE GAME

The event that provoked the ugly word "fix" started in the fall of 1950, when the CAHA created a Major series and the OHA decided in its wisdom to permit Senior B teams to compete for the Allan Cup,

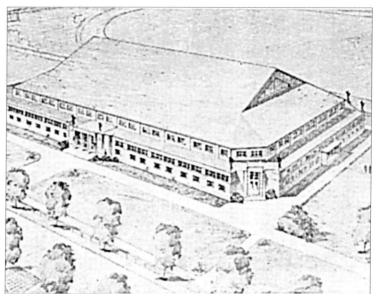

Kingston Community Memorial Centre, Artist's Conception. When the Memorial Centre opened in March 1951, this $350,000 structure featured a 90 by 200 foot ice surface—larger than Maple Leaf Gardens—and was praised as a magnificent facility.

First Goal Scorer, Jack (Mucker) McKeown. Kingston Nylons Jack McKeown scored the first goal when the Kingston Community Memorial Centre was opened in 1951. The historic goal, assisted by Bob Joyce, was captured by a Whig-Standard *photographer (inset).*

emblematic of the Canadian Senior A championship. Little thought was given to this concession as the Kingston entry in the eastern Ontario group, the Nylons, a solid squad of well-tested seniors and a mix of rookies, coached by former professional George (Paddy) Patterson, finished third ahead of Belleville but behind the two Peterborough teams, the Petes and Eagles. The Petes, winners of five out of eight league games against the Nylons, eliminated Kingston three games to one and went on to lose to Owen Sound in the Allan Cup playoffs.

With Kingston attaining the dream of a lifetime on March 6, with the official opening of the new Memorial Centre, the Nylons wracked up record gates in the OHA Senior B playoff with Belleville Redmen. They drew 14,181 fans, or an average of 3,542 for four home dates, and won the series. After two more record crowds against Markham, the Nylons joyfully split the pot, unaware of storm clouds ahead.

It wasn't until the fall when the Nylons split into two camps and entered a second Senior B team for the 1951-52 season that the snow hit the fan. One player admitted the Nylons threw the series against the Petes. The OHA conducted an investigation and suspended the coach and manager for life, two players for two years and 12 for one season. Two were exonerated. It was the blackest day in the history of Kingston hockey.

Overshadowed by these events was the successful start of two other organizations. The Limestone Hockey League, with headquarters in the Jock Harty Arena, was formed for non-OHA players, with 16-year-old Don Boswell as president. Four teams, including a *Whig-Standard* entry, competed each Monday and Wednesday night, using the new enlarged 15-foot face-off circles.

The first hockey games in the new Church Athletic League of Kingston were played in January 1951 under volunteer leadership. The organization was formed on the urging of contractor Harold Harvey, "who knew the hidden power of youth" and felt something should be done to foster and develop their potential good. Eighty-per-cent church or Sunday school attendance was the requirement to qualify for team play. Canon Minto Swan was the first president of the league that would embrace several sports for both boys and girls. Forty years later, the CAL could say: "The dreams of the founders live on with more than 100,000 youngsters being enrolled since its inception."

From the East came news that Kingston grad—George MacGregor—had wound up a five-year career in Nova Scotia senior hockey. Known as "The Playmaker," the smooth skating centreman had averaged 30 goals a season for Glace Bay and Halifax teams. After scoring 234 goals and recording 196

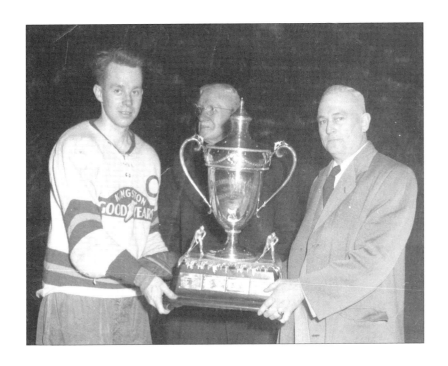

Kingston Goodyears, OHA Senior B Champs, 1952-53 (upper left). Captain George MacGregor, one of the great "money-players" in Kingston, received the championship trophy from Lorne Cook, past president of the provincial association, while James T. Sutherland looked on. The smooth skating centreman was chosen the Goodies' most valuable player and awarded the Ron Plumb Memorial Trophy.

The Champion Goodyears (upper right). Hailed by Whig-Standard cartoonist Joe Paul, this team, sponsored by Tom Disney, drew 90,381 fans to 28 games for a 3,337 average and a record single-game high of 4,870.

Turk Broda's NHL All-Star Softball Team, 1952 (bottom left). Broda's team players were popular visitors to Kingston Penitentiary. Front row: Danny Lewicki, Al Dewsbury, Warden Dick Allan, Turk Broda, Sid Smith; Back row: Hugh Bolton, (Harris), Harry Watson, Johnny McCormick, (Ranasen).

assists, MacGregor left Halifax St. Mary's over "financial difficulties." He was reported to have been the highest paid player in the Maritime Senior League at $160 to $175 a week

1952 BILL COOK NAMED TO HALL OF FAME

The Nylon Social and Athletic Club, rocked by the OHA suspensions, dropped out of senior hockey. A highlight of the season was Montreal Canadiens' 16-4 victory over Kingston and Montreal juniors in a Hall of Fame exhibition game before 3,562 fans at the Memorial Centre.

Kingston fans cheered as Bill Cook, the former New York Ranger super star, was inducted into the Hockey Hall of Fame in Toronto.

1953 "GOODIES" ARE BEST

Kingston Goodyears set some kind of record in winning the OHA Senior B championship in their first season (four games to two over Woodstock, Ontario). Thirteen players—Ted Nicholson, Joe Watts, Bob Londry, Stan Stewart, George MacGregor, Johnny Myke, Jack White, Ken Partis, Jack McKeown, Clint Tinkess, Bud Ohlke and Glynn Udall—were products of Kingston's minor system. John Carr-Harris, another local product, handled the coaching reins, and Joe Corkey was

manager. Belleville Glen Roys, Oshawa Truckers and Toronto Lyndhursts fell before the Goodies' strong attack and Woodstock Athletics went down in six games. A record home crowd of 4,870 cheered on Kingston in the final 12-0 victory.

A special treat this season was a Quebec Junior Hockey League game that was moved from Montreal to Kingston. The incomparable Henri (Pocket Rocket) Richard assisted on the first goal and the winning goal in overtime, as Sam Pollock's Montreal Junior Canadiens edged Montreal Royals 4-3.

Three years after entering junior hockey in Kingston, Don Cherry helped the Barrie Flyers win the Memorial Cup. The future NHL coach scores goals in games four and five against St. Boniface Canadiens.

1954 CAL TEAM TRAVELS

Kingston CAL Peewee all-stars made minor hockey history when the team, under manager Fred Harkness and coach Bill Steen, travelled 300 miles to Goderich in Western Ontario for the Young Canada Tournament and lost in the final to Kitchener. Ed Long, John Harkness and Pete Robertson were among the players that repeated the trip the following season.

Now playing for the Boston Bruins' farm

Kingston Goodyears, OHA Senior B Champions, 1954-55. CKLC's Johnnie Kelly conducted the post-game trophy presentation as captain Ted Nicholson got ready to accept the championship trophy.

team in Hershey, Pennsylvania,, Kingston's Lorne Ferguson lead the AHL with 45 goals and teamed up with Red Sullivan and Dunc Fisher to become the highest scoring line in league history with 286 points.

1955

MAX JACKSON HONOURED

Kingston Goodyears, this time with former Detroit Red Wing Les Douglas as coach and Art Casterton as manager, repeated their OHA Senior B championship of two years ago. The Goodies whipped Whitby Wrens in the group semi-final, ousted Belleville Memos in the group final and won the championship in four straight games over Sarnia Sailors.

Another highlight of the season was the appearance of some of the all-time greats of the game—Nels Stewart, Turk Broda, Dit Clapper and the Conachers, Primeau and Jackson—playing "Reds" versus "Whites," including locals George Patterson and Gus Marker.

Seven Kingston junior hockey players were invited to Montreal for the Canadiens' training camp. They were accompanied by Bill Reason, coach of the Junior Canadiens in the Thousand Islands League and a future NHL scout. And Kingston's Jim Anderson, formerly of Bennett's Barons, was reported to be having a good season

with the American Hockey League Springfield Indians.

This year, Don Cherry played in the only NHL game of his career—a play-off game for Boston in Montreal. The Kingston native went on to an 18-year minor league career and a 480-game NHL coaching career with Boston and Colorado. For the same Bruins team, Lorne Ferguson scored 20 goals, one of just 12 NHL players to reach the 20-goal plateau in the 1954-55 sixty-game season.

Max Jackson was awarded the Ontario Hockey Association's prestigious "Award of Merit" for being the longest serving junior hockey coach in the province—15 seasons coaching the Kingston Junior B Vics.

A hockey beacon went out on September 15, 1955, when Hall of Fame builder James Thomas Sutherland , died in Hotel Dieu Hospital, age 85 and veteran sports columnist Mike Rodden wrote: "Rest easy, Jim . . . because . . .you have left a heritage that is priceless. In this city and this country you will never be forgotten."

1956

THANKS, MR. MARTIN

For the real amateur, the Limestone league supplied spirited action. Len Martin, father of one of the league organizers, Roy (Scotty) Martin, donated a trophy and the first name engraved on it was T.M.

Patterson Mercury's, Limestone City League Champs, 1955-56. Captain Byron Irvine is presented the Len Martin Championship Trophy. Front row: Abby O'Sullivan, Roy (Scotty) Martin, Ron McCormick, Jolly Hewson, Dick Hewson, Ted Wainika; Back row: Harry Patterson, Jim Waddell, Gerry Montgomery, Len Martin, Byron Irvine (C), Moe Mellow, Jack Fraser, Keith Hewson.

J.J. Johnson Motors Saints, Limestone City League Champs, 1956-57. Front row: Johnny Myke, Fuzzy Davis, John Yates, Bill Howland, Ron Lafontaine; Middle row: Jack Johnson (Sponsor), Ed Roddy, Cliff Irwin, Whitey MacClaren, Paddy Koen, Bill Grinrich (Manager), Red Bradley (Coach); Back row: Howie Green, Dennis Ledford, Eddie Rea, Bud Olke, Jim McMahon, Cuth Roy, Len Coyle.

Patterson Mercury's. Mr. Martin presented it for the first time to Byron Irving, captain of the champion Mercury's. Coached by Keith (Tex) Hewson, this club lost only three of 29 games and beat William (Red) Bradley's Saints 3-1 in the final game.

In the late 1950s, an Eastern Ontario Intermediate hockey league was formed with teams from Brockville (Chiefs), Smiths Falls (Bears), Picton (Pirates), Napanee (Comets) and Kingston (Flyers). The Kingston team, said Scotty Martin, featured the better players from the Limestone league, including Ron and Clint Tinkess, Hubert Ball, Don Cole, Jolly Hewson, Tony Pettit, Reg Beatty, Lorne McNeil, Les Ullman, Ellie Gutzman, Tom Meeker, Moe Mellow, John Cook, Wayne Nichols, Charlie Sherman and Dick Dodds, with Doug Finney as general manager and Jack Irvine as coach. Sponsored by Doug Finney and called the 'Flyers," the team was later sponsored by Ace Motors and called "Aces." Down the road, this team would become by the Kingston Senior A Aces.

Elsewhere, Kingston goaltender Bob Senior, after playing all season with the Barrie Flyers, joined the Toronto Marlboros for their Memorial Cup championship win over Regina Pats. For three straight years, Senior's team were beaten out by the eventual cup winners.

1957

THE LCS AND THE SOVIETS

Kingston's new radio station, CKLC, sponsored the Kingston OHA Senior A team. Hub Macey, formerly of Montreal Canadiens and New York Rangers, Don Bellringer and Ted Nicholson were among the veteran stalwarts on the club. Leading scorer Ralph (Bucky) Buchanan was one season away from accidentally losing the sight of one eye in a senior game against Cornwall. The LC's were coached by Fred (Bun) Cook, one of the game's greatest scorers and coaches. Long-time hockey supporter Reg Walton was club president.

The highlight of the second season was the first visit of an overseas team. On Dec. 3, 1957, the Soviets, mostly from Moscow Central Sport Club, easily handled the CKLC All Stars, a team made up of eight Kingston players and augmented by seven from Belleville, Pembroke and Cornwall. It was a difficult night for play-by-play announcer Johnnie Kelly as 17 of the visitors had names ending in "ov," including celebrated defenceman Nikolai Sologubov.

One of the last championship teams to be photographed in the Jock Harty Arena on Arch Street was the J.J. Johnson Motors Saints who captured the Limestone Hockey League crown. Every team member from veterans Johnny Myke and Bud Olke to rookie Len Coyle took home an individual trophy.

Kingston CKLCs, OHA Senior B Champions, 1957-58. Kingston's new radio station sponsored this senior team, managed by Jack Burman and Dick Allan, captained by former pro Hub Macey (front row center), and coached by 'Bun' Cook. The line-up included a mixture of veteran and young players, including Joe Levandoski, Bob Paul, Roy Partridge, Jerry Toppazzini, Bill Colvin, Don Bellringer, Doug Senior, Mike Buchacheski, Ken Linesmen and Ralph (Bucky) Buchanan.

Long-time Kingston hockey official Lorne Cook started a two-year term as president of the Ontario Hockey Association—the first Kingstonian in the position since Capt. James T. Sutherland (1915-17).

The Kingston Midget all-stars, coached by Ken Matthews, upset Toronto in the semi-finals but lost to St. Catharines in the Ontario championship final series. Rising star Doug Senior, the club captain, teamed up with Bud Aylesworth and Doug Mulholland to carry the bulk of the offence for the Kingston kids.

1958

STARS OF TOMORROW

Two thousand spectators attended the Rotary-Kiwanis Minor Hockey Association's "Stars of Tomorrow" night at the Memorial Centre. The kids had a chance to strut their stuff before admiring parents and relatives.

Similar crowds turned out for the CKLC's, particularly when they played the Belleville McFarlands, who went on to the OHA Senior A championship, the Allan Cup and the World Championship in Czechoslovakia. Joe Levandoski, Bob Paul, Roy Partridge, Don Senior, Ken Linsemen, Mike Bukacheski and Jim Anderson were among the LC's best.

1959

PRO HOCKEY COMES TO TOWN

Kingston, a hotbed of amateur hockey since the game was first popularized, made the leap into the professional variety when the Eastern Professional Hockey League was formed in Quebec and Ontario. Sponsored by Boston Bruins with Cal Gardner as playing coach, the club, formerly the Merchants, chose the historic name of Frontenacs. The Kingston Frontenacs took on the Boston colours and instead of the circle B, a circle K. After a training camp in Hull, the Frontenacs lost 4-0 to Boston before 3,646 fans. Stan Maxwell, on relays from Barry Ashbee and Orv Tessier, scored the first goal in professional league history in Kingston as the Frontenacs used the power play to whip Trois Rivieres Lions.

The shortage of artificial ice facilities in the city was spelled out by Harold Harvey, founder of the Church Athletic League, which served 633 boys. The Memorial Centre and Jock Harty Arena, which accommodated 45 CAL and Rotary-Kiwanis teams six years ago, were insufficient he said in urging construction of rink solely for youth up to 18 years. The Rotary-Kiwanis league now offers competition for 255 youths on 17 bantam, midget and juvenile teams.

Frontenac fans welcomed a new player from Boston, Willy O'Ree, who the previous year became

Good Sports. Kingston's Doug Senior and future NHLer Ray Cullen of St. Catharines Lions exchange congratulations following the championship game, with OMHA officials Ash Morrison, Jack Christie and Frank Doherty standing by.

Kingston Midgets, OMHA Finalists, 1957. Coach Ken Matthews' midget team came up just short in their quest for the Ontario title against St. Catharines. Front row: Merritt Decker, Bob Holland, Bob Shephard, Doug Senior, Ken Matthews (coach), Dennis O'Donnell, Peter Kane; Back row: Tom Pettit, trainer, Dennis Amey, Bill Napier, Sid Faulkner, Bud Aylesworth, John Jarvis, John Gibson, John Tuttle, (not identified), Garnett Ball, Doug Mulholland, Roger Shea.

the first black to play in the NHL. The 25-year-old Fredericton, New Brunswick native scored 20 goals in 60 games for the Fronts and went back to the Bruins and compiled 14 points in 43 games but spent the rest of his career in the Western League.

1960 NEW ARENA FOR RMC

The opening of a $350,000, 400-seat arena by Royal Military College relieved the ice rental situation in Kingston and boosted hockey and skating in the Fort Henry Heights, Barriefield area. Named after the late Maj.-Gen. C.F. Constantine, a decorated war veteran and former commandant and hockey player, the rink was officially opened January 24.

The Frontenacs were the talk of the town and the whole region. Despite a record-shattering season by centre Orval Tessier —59 goals and 67 assists in 70 games—and 93 points by Cal Gardner, the Fronts finished last behind Sudbury, Montreal, Hull-Ottawa, Trois-Rivieres and Sault Ste. Marie.

A month after the 1959-60 season closed, Frontenac vice-president Jim Magee announced the signing of Wren Blair as coach and general manager. Hailed as a moulder of champions, the former Whitby Dunlop mentor would assure exciting and winning times in the decade ahead.

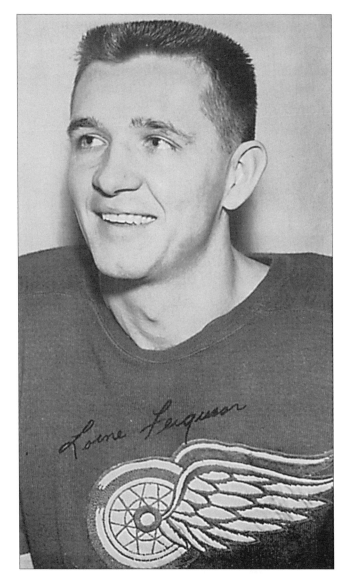

Lorne Ferguson. A 20-goal scorer with the Bruins the previous year, Lorne Ferguson helped the Detroit Red Wings win the 1956 Stanley Cup final against Montreal. He played eight NHL seasons with Boston, Detroit and Chicago.

Kingston Frontenacs, Eastern Professional Hockey League, 1959-60. The Frontenacs joined the EPHL as the city's first professional hockey team, a farm team of the Boston Bruins. Front row: Howard Jacques, Skip Teal, Cal Gardner (coach), Reg Fleming, Wayne Nichols; Middle row: Nelson Bullock, Orval Tessier, Don McLeod, Stan Maxwell, Barry Krake, Barry Ashbee; Back row: Bun Cook (trainer), Buddy Boone, Willy O'Ree, Don Anderson, Glenn Cressman, Gerry (Red) Ouelette, John Carr-Harris (General Manager). Insets: Bob Blackburn, Pete Panagabko.

Minor Hockey
A Major Sport

HOCKEY HAS BEEN A treasured activity for Kingston boys since the days of free wheeling shinny on the harbour ice. A century ago a boys' hockey league was first organized and a trophy donated for the winner. It started with a juvenile association and grew into midget and bantam age divisions.

Service clubs organized the first leagues during the depressed 1930s. No boy was turned away. One group was called The Welfare League. Rotarians, Iranians and Lions were in the forefront and the organized activity grew into the RKMHA. The Church Athletic League, Young Nationals, Lakeshore Hockey Association, Kingston Township and Greater Kingston associations followed. All-star or "rep" teams have taken the Kingston name to the highest of honours in the Ontario Minor and Ottawa District hockey association competitions. In the past 15 years, the girls of Kingston and Frontenac have developed their own competitions, winning provincial laurels, and some of the players have achieved national and Olympic international recognition.

To recognize and salute the rich history of youth hockey, the following photo album is dedicated to young people and the hundreds of anonymous adults who made it possible.

Two New Kingston Arenas Opened in 1968. (Top) Syl Apps joins Bill and 'Bun' Cook at the official opening of the Cook Brother's Arena, and (below) federal cabinet minister Edgar Benson (left) and Syl Apps (far right) congratulate Wally Elmer and his wife Inez on the opening of the Wally Elmer Youth Centre.

Harold Harvey, Founder of the Church Athletic League.

Church Athletic League Players, 1957. Every child was given an equal opportunity to play.

Kingston Saints, Midget Champions, 1941-42. Bill Reason's team brought Kingston its first Ontario Minor Hockey championship. First row: Ed Plumb, Ted Fowler, Bud Aitken, Doug Smart, Jack Gibson, George Cotman, Elmer Johnson Dave Silliman; Back row: James de St. Remy (Sponsor), Bill Mills (Mgr), Phil Metcalfe, Fred Gurnsey, Jack Stephenson, Graham Donaghue, Jeff Coleman, Bill Moore, Bill Reason (Coach), Bill Frayne (Trainer).

Church Athletic League Peewees, 1956-57. Don (Pete) Petersen (front row centre) had great success with his CAL Pee Wee all-stars. Leo Lavallee, Danny White, Jim Sprott, Brian Roe, Johnny Mercer and goaltender Bob Benson would help win the Central Ontario Championship in 1958.

St. Michaels Separate School, Separate School Hockey League Champions, 1958-59. The Pee Wee team from this school in Portsmouth village went through an undefeated season and surrendered just one goal the entire year!

Rotary Kiwanis Juveniles, Ontario Finalists, 1963-64. Dick Cherry's juvenile all-stars were finalists at the All Ontario Juvenile championships. Front row: John Coates, Don Goodridge, Mike Carson, Brian Roe, John Osborne, Scott Irvine, Larry Giguere; Second row: Jack Irvine (Asst Mgr), Drew Kennedy, Terry Landon, Pat Catlin, Earl Routly, Dennis McCullough, Carl Neilson, Dave Carr-Harris, Dick Cherry (Coach), Harry Kennedy (Mgr); Back row: Rick Williamson, Jack Watts, Jim Beveridge, Leo Lavallee, Ed Leeman, Phil McCann

Ernestown Township Amherstview Lions, OMHA Atom B Champs, 1988-89. Jay McKee, a future NHL defenceman, and Ryan Vince, who broke scoring records for the Kingston Township Voyageurs in the 1990s, played on this team. Front Row: Jacen Douglas, Ryan Vince, Steve Gendron, Jeff Turney, Andrew McDonald, Josh Jones; Middle Row: Steve McAuley, Kevin McCormick, Michael Grawberger, Jay McKee, Steve Kiley, Troy Moon, Jeff Treleaven, Jason Withers; Back Row: Ron Turney (Trainer), Jim Gendron (Manager), Bill Vince (Coach), Gord McKee (Asst Coach).

Ernestown Jets, OMHA Bantam B Champions, 1978-79. Before he was "hip", Gord Downie, lead singer for The Tragically Hip rock band, was a goalie for the Ernestown bantam team that captured the Ontario championship. Front row: Richard Abbott, Gord Downie, Phillip Bunsick, Vern Draper, Rick Chard; Middle row: Andy McGrogen (Trainer), Paul McGrogen, Mike Kelly, Troy MacPhail, Myron Kramer, Kenny Hartwick, Jack Orwell (Manager), Reg Buss (Coach); Back row: Trevor Kramer, Richard Buss, Kevin Hartwick, Randy Gilmour.

Kingston Kodiaks, Ontario Pee Wee B Champions, 1988-89. The Kodiaks won numerous provincial titles in the 1980s and '90s. Coach Beth Duff is front and centre on this team that was led by future Olympic star Jayna Hefford. Front row: Christina Johnson, Jennifer Wright, Karen VanLuven, Lynn Connery, Wendy MacDonald, Alison Kelly; Back row: Sandra Hefford (Mgr), Jenny Rawson, Sarah Bartsch, Janet Craigen, Karen Kendall, Jayna Hefford, Laura McCurdy, Shellie Bender, Kathy VanLuven, Pam Harvey, Sarah Kisilevesky, Steve Wright (Asst Coach).

Kingston Young Nats Pee Wees, North American Silver Stick Champions, 1971. Coached by Dr. Gerry Wagar, this team enjoyed an amazing season, 50-wins, 2-losses and one tie, capped off by winning the championship in Port Huron, Michigan. Front row: Ricky Coupland, Neil Faulkner, Brian Clancy, Barry Wood, Kevin Taylor, Darrell Westcott; Second row: Walt Westcott (Mgr), Cam MacGregor, Mike Simurda, Bill Jenkins, Roger Marshall, Rick Paterson, Gerry Wagar (Coach); Back row: Reg Walton, Tim Torrance, Mike Koresky, Kenny Linseman, Terry Wagar (Asst Coach).

CHAPTER EIGHT

The Surprising Sixties

Hockey moved into high gear at all levels in the 1960s, thanks mainly to the impetus of a winning professional team and the awareness that the recreational game needed expanded facilities. Two new arenas were built by the city, and its youth never had it so good for practice and playing time.

With the Frontenacs playing in a development league (only two players over 25), Kingston saw players that would star in the NHL in the late '60s and early '70s. When the pros attained championship form and then departed, "community hockey" took over with teams mixing Kingston talent with experienced veterans. Three more provincial championships, two in one season, were attained by Kingston clubs, and local talent started to move in numbers into play-for-pay circuits.

Women's hockey rebounded—at least at Queen's—as the Women's Intercollegiate Athletic Union reintroduced the game to its sports agenda.

And in what other community would a park be named after a former NHL referee, Mike Rodden, and three streets called after NHL

The Church Athletic League Rink. An open air, natural ice rink when it was constructed in Portsmouth village in the 1950s, this rink had artificial ice installed for the 1961-62 season and was later enclosed and named the Harold Harvey Recreation Centre in honour of the CAL founder.

stars, Lionel Conacher (Drive), Howie Morenz (Crescent) and James Sutherland (Drive) in (Gus) Marker's Acres?

1961 MIDGETS TOPS IN OMHA

The Frontenacs moved up two rungs on the EPHL ladder in their second season, just grabbing the last playoff spot by one point over Sudbury. The team lost Orval Tessier to the Bruins for half the season, but manager Wren Blair recruited top Whitby amateur Bobby Attersley, who responded with 66 points in 64 games. Stan Maxwell, George (Goose) Gosselin, Dick Meissner and Buddy Boone provided additional playmaking and sniping power. Harry Sinden was a tower of strength on defence. One of the Fronts' peskiest opponents was Kingston-born Don Cherry of Kitchener-Waterloo.

The 1,000-strong CAL membership met its own demand for ice time when a new rink was opened in a former Portsmouth rock quarry and dedicated to its founder, construction magnate Harold Harvey. The $150,000 structure called for a two-storey clubhouse and open-air ice surface. The project, with the aid of a $50,000 city grant, was financed and built in one year. President E.H. (Ebby) Hare, a prime mover in the project, said Kingston was the smallest community in Canada with such an outdoor facility. Toronto has 28,

Montreal 19 and Ottawa nine.

The strong Rotary-Kiwanis RKMHA league (the Hawks, Huskies Elks, Panthers, etc.), plus the CAL feeder group, finally paid off in a provincial hockey title. The OMHA Midget A all-stars, coached by Garry Young, eliminated Belleville and Oshawa and ousted Stamford 7-5 and 4-3 to win the Stafford Trophy. Gary Lavallee, a hard-skating centreman, paced the team in the stretch drive with 17 goals, including two in one overtime period. Also catching the eyes of scouts was wiry winger Wayne Cashman and hard-driving Charlie Convery.

Meanwhile in the NHL, Art Casterton became the first and only Kingston official to referee in the league. In the late 1950s and early 1960s, besides working NHL games, Casterton saw plenty of action refereeing in the EPHL and the AHL and also handled games in the Memorial Cup, Allan Cup and Calder Cup finals.

1962 ACTION ON "TWO FRONTS"— PRO AND AMATEUR

The third Frontenac pro squad faced all kinds of adversity but didn't like to lose. Blair signed three rookies from training camp, picked up Bob Olajos and Dick Cherry on loan, added American Olympic star Tommy Williams and purchased high-scoring Tom McCarthy. The team fell just four

Bob Olajos and Bob Leiter, Kingston Frontenacs. Shown in this promotional photo, these two players were members of the 1963 Eastern Professional Hockey League championship team.

Harry Sinden. This smooth defenseman doubled as an Assistant Coach with the 1963 champion Kingston Frontenacs. The former Amherstview resident went on to a successful coaching and management career with the Boston Bruins, coached Team Canada in 1972, and was inducted into the Hockey Hall of Fame.

Pat (Whitey) Stapleton. This offensive defenceman was one of the most popular players with the Frontenacs championship team, compiling 39 points in 46 games, earning him a return to the Boston Bruins. He later starred for Chicago Black Hawks and played for Team Canada in 1972.

Bruce Gamble. This popular goaltender backstopped the Frontenacs during their championship season and played 10 years in the NHL.

Orval Tessier. Twice a 50-goal scorer with the Frontenacs, Tessier set an EPHL scoring record in 1959-60 with 59 goals and 129 points. He later coached the Cornwall Royals and Chicago Black Hawks.

points shy of taking first place. Sparked by Tessier's 54 goals and McCarthy's 53 markers and 60-plus assist efforts by Attersley and Sinden, the Fronts eliminated Sudbury in the semi-finals but lost 4-2 in games to Hull-Ottawa, which won the last game in double overtime.

Kingston's Lorne Ferguson, after a 442-game career in the NHL, returned here and played two seasons—his playing time cut in half by nagging injuries and a 25-stitch skate cut.

In the amateur limelight were the Kingston Junior Frontenacs, who won the last 12 games of their schedule to enter an OHA round-robin competition. Coached by Danny McLeod, the team was led by lanky Wayne Cashman with a solid lineup that included Gary McMillan, Charlie Convery, Pete Robertson, Bob Rawson, Fred Curran, Gary Lavallee, Garfield Ball and Kurt Demmler. The following year the club won the Eastern league title and went to the quarter-finals before losing to Lakeshore Bruins.

1963 KINGSTON'S ONLY PRO CHAMPIONSHIP

The Junior Frontenacs returned with their line-up intact and eliminated Peterborough Monsens, Toronto Lakeshore Goodyears and Burlington Braves to claim the Red Sullivan Trophy. Despite a valiant effort in the Junior B provincial finals against St. Mary's Lincolns, Danny McLeod's team went down four games to two. Battling to the end were players who would shine in senior and professional hockey—Ron Earl, Gary Lavallee, Garfield Ball, Guy White and Wayne Cashman. "For our money," said realtor Ross McMahon in a quarter-page newspaper ad, "You're still the champs!"

With the EPHL down to four teams and assistant coach Harry Sinden second to Gerry Ouellette in scoring, the Frontenacs finished in first place, seven points up on Hull-Ottawa Canadiens. St. Louis, with Gananoque's Pete Ford solid on defence, finished fourth and Hull-Ottawa, with Kingston's Doug Senior a scoring threat, lost to third-place Sudbury in the semifinals.

Kingston captured the EPHL championship and the Tom Foley Trophy by ousting the Wolves in five games, 4-1. Cliff Pennington, Dick Cherry and Don Blackburn led the team in scoring. Pat Stapleton was strong both ways on defence, and Bruce Gamble was a standout in goal.

At the end of the season sportswriter Allan Dickie quoted Wren Blair thusly: "I have to sit down with our people in Boston and decide the future of our EPHL organization —whether to remain in Kingston or move to the United States." The answer was not long in coming. The league shuffled off to the U.S. and became the Central

Kingston Junior B Frontenacs, Eastern Ontario Champs, 1964. Bob Senior replaced Danny McLeod as coach following the team's trip to the '63 Ontario finals, and, helped by two future NHLers—Dennis Kearns and Rick Smith—they won the Eastern Ontario title. Front row: Bob Benson, Gary MacMillan, Guy White, Bob Senior (coach), Gary Lavallee (captain), Fred Harkness (manager), Ron Earl, Charlie Convery, Neil Perry; Second row: Jim Magee, Don Smith, Doug Percival, Barry White, Rick Smith, Wayne Clancy, Doc Myles; Back row: Bill Steen, Danny White, Rick Eaton, John Mercer, Mike McMahon, Dennis Kearns, Bob Bruce, John Knox.

Hockey League with the Kingston-Boston players moving to Minneapolis.

1964 JUNIOR B CHAMPS

Bob Senior replaced Danny McLeod behind the bench and the Kingston Junior Frontenacs went on to win the Eastern Ontario Junior B title. The team repeated the regional honour in 1969.

Former Kingston and Peterborough junior, Doug Senior, had his best year in pro hockey with the league champion Omaha Knights of the CHL, scoring 32 goals and adding 43 assists for 75 points in 72 games. Also performing well with the Knights was another Kingston product, Tom Carty.

1965 EX-PROS BOOST ACES

Lorne Ferguson made a comeback with the Kingston Aces and together with Dick Cherry's reinstatement to the amateur ranks and Tom Carty's release from Eddie Shore's Springfield Indians, the OHA Senior club had three proven pros.

The CAL, now 81-teams strong, celebrated this year when a roof with new lighting was constructed over its outdoor artificial ice surface. Next door to the Memorial Centre, a new building, constructed in 1961, opened its doors as the International

Hockey Hall of Fame with local minor hockey coach Garry Young as curator. The shrine, officially granted to Kingston in 1943, was contained on the second floor of the $140,000 city-owned building. Admission was 25 cents.

1966 MERCHANTS COME CLOSE

A team organized in 1964 as the Gananoque-Kingston Merchants to play in the Eastern Ontario Intermediate league hit pay dirt this season. Coached by Ted Walton, this group of scrappy underdogs went to the OHA Intermediate A final and lost a two-game series to Dundas.

1967 CELEBRATING CANADA'S BIRTHDAY

During Canada's Centennial Year, the focus was on Kingston for a couple of reasons. The Limestone City was selected by the Canadian Amateur Hockey Association as the site of the first national midget tournament. Teams from 10 provinces and two territories were billeted in Kingston homes, and over a week-long period Toronto Butter Beeps, representing Ontario, defeated Alberta (Edmonton Centennials) to win the championship. Such future NHLers as Bob Kelly, Randy Rota and Orest Kindrachuck got their first national exposure before several pro scouts here.

Kingston Aces, OHA Senior A Champions and Allan Cup Finalists, 1967. Front row: Tom Mercer, Jim Gebhardt, Gord Leach, Bill Burega (captain), Joe King, Charles Convery, Neil Perry; Second row: A. McKenzie, Bob Rawson, Davey Jones, Peter Weston, Jim Sprott, Bob Olajos, Dennis Kearns, Bob Brown, Glynn Udall, Major Danny McLeod (coach); Back row: Pat Driscoll, Garnett Ball, Ed Long, Tom Carty, John Ford, Bob Collins, Jerry Polywkan. Missing: Ron Earl.

Senior hockey fans had their eyes on the Aces. Danny McLeod's club won the OHA Senior A championship easily over Woodstock Alcans and took Morrisburg in Allan Cup playoffs before losing to Drummondville Eagles in the Eastern Canada semi-finals. This was a gutsy, well-balanced club. Three members—captain Bill Burega, Tom Carty and Bob Olajos—had professional experience, and two of the rookies—Syl Apps, Jr. and Dennis Kearns—would establish careers in the NHL, while Rod Graham would move to the AHL.

The league-leading Aces left Christmas Day for their first overseas jaunt—a three-week tour of Switzerland and Sweden. Led by 37-year-old ex-NHLers Lorne Ferguson, but missing pro-bound Dennis Kearns and teacher Tom Carty, Kingston lost 2-0 to Moscow Locomotive, beat Finland, 3-1, and blanked Switzerland, 2-0. In 14-degree weather, for the Spengler Cup, the Aces played one bad period in the final and lost 8-4 to the Soviets. In Sweden, the Canadians won three games, including a wild, battle royal in Stockholm. Police were called on to the ice, nine major penalties were handed to nine Aces, including Syl Apps, Jr., Bill Burega, Ron Earl, and Bob Olajos, who was suspended for the rest of the tour.

Kingston Merchants, a late entry in the OHA Senior B league, played 11 exhibition games with several teams, including Oshawa and Peterborough,

that withdrew from the provincial competition. This 100-per-cent local club, with one championship to its credit, scored 11-7 and 6-4 victories over Wallaceburg, which had ousted Windsor and Kitchener, to give Kingston the rare distinction of holding two OHA Senior championships in the same year.

Elsewhere in 1967, the Oklahoma City Blazers, formed from the transplanted EPHL Kingston Frontenacs, win back- to-back championship in the Central Hockey League (1966-1967). The Blazers' line-up included Harry Sinden, Dick Cherry, Wayne Cashman and former Frontenacs Pete Panagabko and J.P. Parise.

LAVALLEEMEN LEAD WAY

With basically the same lineup as the previous year, Walton's Merchants won the OHA Intermediate A championship (Kingston's last), this time over Brantford, 14-9 on goals. Only a strong club from Kapuskasing in northern Ontario stopped the Merchants from going to the Canadian final. Leo Lavallee, Jim Stinson, Les Colligan and army recruit Wally Travis paced the forwards while Dennis O'Donnell and captain Gary Lavallee anchored the defence in front of Wayne Nichols and Dave Gavel.

Gary Lavallee, just seven years after leading the midget all-stars to a provincial championship,

Rick Smith and Bob Pulford, 1965. Kingston defenceman Rick Smith receives the championship trophy from Bob Pulford at a midget hockey tournament in Trenton. Before the end of the decade, they would face one another in the NHL.

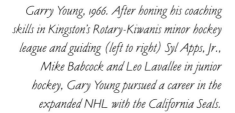

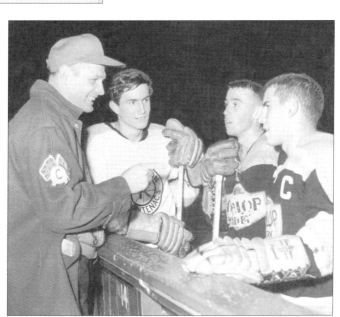

Garry Young, 1966. After honing his coaching skills in Kingston's Rotary-Kiwanis minor hockey league and guiding (left to right) Syl Apps, Jr., Mike Babcock and Leo Lavallee in junior hockey, Gary Young pursued a career in the expanded NHL with the California Seals.

Jim Dorey, 1968. This Kingston native established a single-game record for penalties in his NHL debut with the Toronto Maple Leafs.

coached the Kingston midget all-stars to the new triple-A division title. The RKMHA Selects edged Sarnia 4-3 before 2,025 at the Memorial Centre as Mike Lynch scored one goal and passed for three others. Against Toronto Marlies for the Ontario title, the Lavalleemen came close, losing 4-2 in Toronto and 4-3 in overtime at home. On the winners was Glenn Goldup, son of Kingston-born pro Hank Goldup.

Kingston's production line was in high gear. Three potential pros—Bruce Landon, Dave Gilmour and Ron Plumb—all played for Peterborough Petes in a pre-season game in Kingston against Ottawa 67s.

There was a certain nostalgic sadness this season as the old Jock Harty Arena on Arch Street in the centre of the Queen's University campus was torn down to make way for the expanding university. Last used for hockey in 1967, the razing sounded the death knell of the old Limestone league.

Balancing this loss was news of three major projects. The CAL raised $20,000, including $5,000 from the Flying Fathers benefit game, to enclose the sides of the Harold Harvey Recreation Centre, where parents and fans had shivered outside or peeped through frosty windows to watch the action at the outdoor ice. The project left the CAL with a modern rink valued at $250,000.

Thanks to the city's parks and recreation department, Kingston's hockey and skating facilities were doubled late in the year with the opening of the Cook Brothers Youth Centre, named after Kingstonians Bill and Bun Cook, stars of the NHL, and the Wally Elmer Youth Centre, which honoured Wally Elmer, long-time professional player and amateur coach and sports benefactor in Kingston.

Jim Dorey made a memorable debut with Toronto Maple Leafs by setting a total penalty record in his first game and ending up with 200 minutes on the year, second in the NHL. The rugged rearguard was also strong offensively earning 30 points in 61 games.

Jim Gebhardt of Kingston Aces and Wally Travis of RMC opened the season drilling Toronto Maple Leafs with medicine balls and heavy shells at the NHL team's training camp at Peterborough.

A highlight of the fourth year of the Kingston Merchants Hockey Club under president Josh Nichols and manager Len Coyle was an international game with a speedy, finely trained Seibu team from Japan. Playing out of the Wally Elmer Youth Centre, the Waltonmen competed in their final year against Cobourg, Wellington, Campbellford, Picton and Napanee.

Bob Londry suffered a separated shoulder as Kingston Old Timers defeated the Flying Fathers, 11-7, in a CAL benefit game before a capacity

Kingston Merchants, OHA Senior B Champs, 1966-67. The Merchants joined the Aces as Centennial year champs winning the OHA Senior B title. The following year, with virtually the same lineup, they captured the provincial Intermediate A championship. Front row: Ted Walton (coach), Peter Robert, Gary Lavallee, Wayne Nichols, B. Stewart, Josh Nichols (Pres); Second row: Harold Langabeer (Mgr) Bob Bruce, Brian Roe, Paul O'Sullivan, Dennis O'Donnell, Wayne Dowdell; Top row: Jim Stinson, G. Hynes, R. Beggs, Tom Pettit, Len Coyle, B. Murphy. Absent, Les Colligan, Fred Curran.

Memorial Centre crowd. Bud Aitken, John Myke and Don Senior led the winners with two goals apiece.

Kingston Bantam Elks, coached by Ed Plumb and managed by Bill Steen, defeated the New York Presidents at the Riverdale Skating Club in New York City. The winner's lineup included Barry Ashby, Rob Plumb, Kevin Treacy, Kirk Twigg and Mike Steacy.

1970 CHEERS FOR CAL

The Church Athletic League marked its 20th birthday and the Kingston Frontenac Rotary Club contributed to the league half the gate from a crowd of 3,554 that attended an exhibition game. All eyes were on Maurice (Rocket) Richard who scored four goals as Montreal's ex-Canadiens defeated Max Jackson's Kingston Oldtimers, including Orv Tessier and 64-year-old William (Bump) Watts.

The decade closed with the opening of yet another new ice sports facility for Kingston. Queen's, the first university in Canada to have its own arena, had been without one for the past four years. In October it unveiled the Jock Harty Arena III as part of a $6-million athletic complex. With a 190-by-85-foot ice surface and seating for 1,800, the rink was opened for hockey when future professional Morris Mott led the Golden Gaels over the University of Buffalo. A few months later, Syl Apps, Minister of Correctional Services and a former Toronto Maple Leaf star, officially opened the structure.

The hockey ice time situation was further improved in the area when Kingston Township opened its first artificial ice rink, appropriately named "Centre 70" at Reddendale. The facility gave great impetus to the township minor hockey association originally launched as Lakeshore Athletic League by Burlington expatriate Reg Locke.

Kingston Aces, coached by Danny McLeod, finished in third place in the OHA Senior League but were tops in attendance with a season's average of 2,213.

In the NHL, the Boston Bruins won their first Stanley Cup since 1941 with a strong Kingston connection. Coach Harry Sinden, forward Wayne Cashman and defenceman Rick Smith. In the cup-clinching game, Smith scored the Bruins first goal and Bobby Orr tallied his famous overtime winner against St. Louis. Cashman and Smith were feted by 500 fans at the International Hockey Hall of Fame.

Ron Plumb of the Peterborough Petes was named the top defenceman in the OHA Junior A and was Boston's first round pick in the NHL draft.

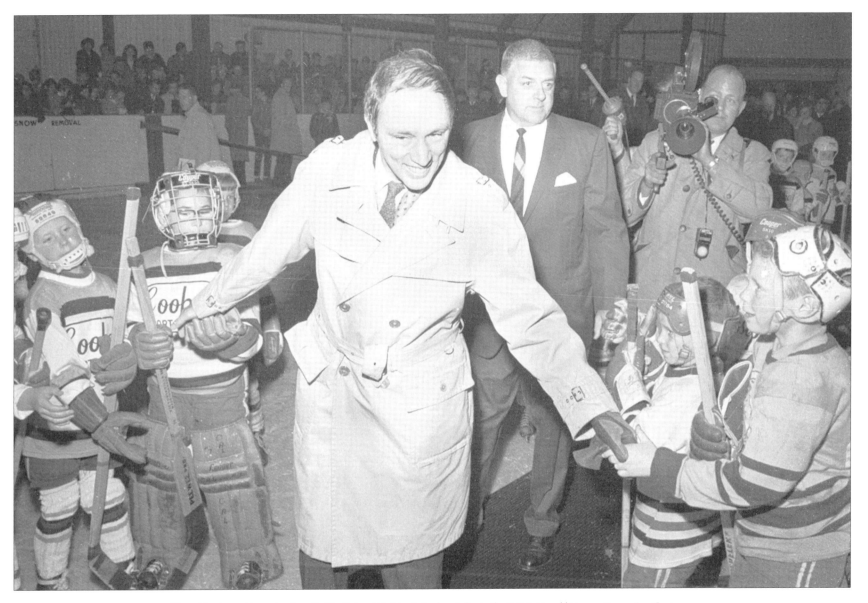

Pierre Trudeau , November 8, 1968. The Prime Minister helped re-dedicate the CAL's Harold Harvey Recreation Centre, escorted by CAL President E.J. (Ted) Fowler.

Historic *Hockey* Series

A History Lesson on Ice

FOR OVER 30 WINTERS, a group of hardy Kingstonians have gathered—or attempted to gather—on the frozen shores of the city harbour to celebrate a special occasion. It's called "historic hockey,' a re-enactment or commemoration of the first organized stick-ball game played on skates in Kingston in 1886. The games are played in a unique setting in the shadow of Kingston's prestigious mid-19th century City Hall.

This spectacle owes its longevity to two great educational institutions, the Royal Military College of Canada and Queen's University at Kingston, whose students introduced a new game to the Limestone City with a series of annual matches. It grew into a three-team, round-robin series with the aid of the Royal Canadian Horse Artillery Regiment, which represented the garrison teams that had played an early version of hockey or shinny on the harbour ice dating back to 1843.

The revival of the first "organized game" of 1886 occurred in 1969, when the Kingston Winter Carnival needed a lively focal point for it mid-winter program. It came about because of the vision and dedication of Phil Quattrocchi, a vibrant Italo-Canadian businessman who organized and promoted the first winter carnivals in the city in the 1960s. He was aided and abetted

by John Tett, Kingston's first recreation director, and the RCHA Brigade Association, whose members supplied a unique trophy for the winning team. It displayed an old clip-on, spring skate and a replica of Victoria or Shoal Tower, the limestone sentinel that overlooks the site where the first game was played and subsequent re-enactments were held—weather permitting.

Not even the construction of a multi-slip marina along the Confederation Park shoreline or atrocious ice conditions over the years could kill this annual celebration of Canada's national winter sport. Traditional January thaws have played havoc with outdoor ice surfaces, and seven times the annual games had to be moved indoors. On one occasion, mild weather forced organizers to switch the action to an outdoor park rink where the ice was so soft that some of the players were muddied and players cavorted around on boots.

The International Hockey Hall of Fame, which became sole sponsor of the Historic Hockey Series in 1972, has attempted to make the re-enactment as authentic as possible. Early rules were researched and efforts made to duplicate the seven-man game, complete with centres using short field hockey type sticks facing the side of the rink, no forward passing and lots of lifting or icing of the puck. Goaltenders, unprotected by heavy pads, were penalized for kneeling or lying on the ice. Only the lack of old-time skates spoiled the illusion of the pioneer game. It was an all-male game until the 1990s, when Queen's, selecting players from its fourth year phys-ed classes, introduced two or three female players. The co-ed style has been following by the other two competitors.

During the bone-chilling weather or the perfect sunny days on the waterfront, the spirit of the gentlemen cadets, the tam-o-shanter topped students and the husky soldiers of the 2nd

Historic Hockey, 1984. Queen's students and RMC cadets duplicate everything but early skates in their annual clash on the natural ice in front of Victoria (Shoal) Tower on the Kingston waterfront. The object of pursuit is a square puck—similar to the one used in the first game in 1886.

Regiment RCHA from Petawawa has shone through. Using short, field hockey type sticks, they have duelled and crashed in attempting to shoot the bouncing square puck through two uprights frozen in the ice. And sometimes in their exuberant play, offenders of the simple rules have caught the attention of the bell-ringing referee who sent them to the "cooler"—a spot in the snowbank on the sidelines.

After two 10-minute periods, playing against the wind or with the sun in their eyes, the victors have emerged, college or regimental yells have been shouted, and the winning trophy paraded around the snow and ice-chipped surface in a ceremony reminiscent of the Stanley Cup ritual. Few of the hardy spectators who survive the chilly afternoon have had the pleasure of attending the joyous post-game festivities in the nearby clubrooms of the RCHA Brigade Association. There, after cups of hot chilli and cool brew, winners and runners-up have mingled and shared stories with special guests —ex-professionals, whose recalled the delights of hockey when participation—the sheer fun and novelty of the event—was the prize.

At this event, the main trophy is hoisted again, MVP awards are presented and, most importantly, a special award is presented to the official who had contributed to the event off the ice. It was named in memory of historic hockey founder, Phil Quattrocchi, whose life as a community servant and booster was tragically ended in a motor vehicle accident. The memory of this unique gentleman—in tuque and coon-skinned coat—spreading joy and sometimes sips of homemade wine lives on in the annual award for distinguished service. The series also commemorates the contribution of its earliest referee, the late Jim Couvell. An award has been made in his name to the most valuable player in the series.

Throughout the third of a century of Historic Hockey, while a lusty, competitive attitude prevails, a special spirit of fun has reigned throughout. The RMC cadets dominated in the early years, Queen's came to the forefront later and in the last decade, the RCHA regiment has dominated the action. In the end, the statistics proved how it all evened out over the years. Not counting the inaugural year when only two teams competed, the Cadets have recorded 14 wins and Queens and RCHA, 10 wins apiece. Being able to say, "I played in the Historic Hockey Series," rather than "We won the cup," appeared to be more important in the long run.

As Kingston's Edward R. Grenda has commented: "Why Historic Hockey? The annual re-enactment and competition is an opportunity for us to appreciate and capture a fleeting glimpse of the growth and development of hockey. The game did not come upon the Canadian winter scene full born. It did not just happen. There were numerous enthusiastic and dedicated officials, sponsors, organizers and players who devoted year to restructuring the rules and developing equipment and facilities. The result is that we now have a colourful, thrilling sport spectacle that is comfortably enjoyed indoors. Historic Hockey is then a history lesson brought to life; a reminder of our debts to our predecessors and a competition bundled into one package."

Historic Hockey has been the main outreach of the International Hockey Hall of Fame and Museum since 1972. The spectacle, including pre-game and post-game activities, has cost thousands of dollars and kept the museum name front and center. Besides the vagaries of the weather, the insurance and safety regulation requirements, this unique "history lesson on ice" series may have reached its final stage. Whether it continues as a rare antidote to the February blahs depends on the several intangibles

Trophy Winners. Royal Military College cadets proudly display the RCHA Brigade Association trophy after winning the Historic Hockey Series on Kingston harbour ice in 1972.

Ken Dryden, February 11, 1989. Hall of Fame goaltender Ken Dryden experienced Historic Hockey in Kingston when he donned size 12 police boots with ancient spring clip-on skates to play forward for Royal Military College cadets.

Gunners of 2nd Regiment Royal Canadian Horse Artillery. CFB Petawawa gunners announce each Historic Hockey goal by firing a nine-pound canon.

and whether there is the spirit or survival equal to the energy, vision and perseverance of its founder. The spirit and vitality to keep the event going was evident in February 2003, when RMC cadets dropped out and RMC ex-cadet veterans and KCVI students filled the void. Who will step forward in 2004?

THE HISTORIC HOCKEY RECORD

Year	Champions
1969	Queen's
1970	4 RCHA
1971	RMC
1972	RMC
1973	RMC
1974	RMC
1975	RMC
1976	2 RCHA
1977	RMC
1978	Queen's
1979	RMC
1980	Queen's
1981	Queen's
1982	Queen's
1983	RMC
1984	2 RCHA
1985	RMC
1986	Queen's
1987	Queen's
1988	2 RCHA
1989	Queen's
1990	RMC
1991	2 RCHA
1992	Queen's
1993	Queen's
1994	2 RCHA
1995	Queen's
1996	2 RCHA
1997	RMC
1998	RMC
1999	2 RCHA
2000	RMC
2001	2 RCHA
2002	2 RCHA
2003	RMC Ex-Cadets

The Phil Quattrocchi Memorial Award Winners

1994—Don Haylock, RCHA Brigade
1995—Bill Fitsell, statistician
1996—Len Coyle, referee
1997—Art Casterton, head referee
1998—Mark Potter, announcer
1999—Doug Clark, goal judge
2000—Sean Moyles, 2 RCHA
2001—Ed Grenda, chairman
2002—Rolf Lund & Ed Deans, Queen's
2003—Chuck Burns, RCHA Brigade.

Jim Couvell Memorial M.V.P. Award Winners

1992—Colin Norris, Queen's
1993—Don Durno, Queen's
1994—Steve Drover, 2 RCHA
1995—Ken Butler, Queen's
1996—Brian MacPherson, 2 RCHA
1997—Chris Stawson, Queen's
1998—Bob Mitchell, RMC
1999—Ron Laurin 2 RCHA
2000—Greg Bono, 2 RCHA
2001—Bobby Hall, 2 RCHA
2002—Rod Gallant, 2 RCHA
2003—Kevin Horsman, RMC Ex-Cadets

Kingston Canadians, 1973-74. Major Junior A hockey arrived in Kingston as the Canadians begin their inaugural season. Front row: John Humphries (trainer), Mike Freeman, Greg Holst, Jack 'Red" Bowness (coach), Gord Buynak (captain), Jim Magee (Pres), Mike O'Connell, Walter 'Punch' Scherer (GM), Brad Rhiness, Steve Dine, Len Coyle (Asst Trainer); Second row: Michael Simurda (Exec-Dir), Eric Brubacker, Kip Acton, Larry Murphy, Barry Scully, John Bialas, John Fielding, Mark Suzor, Peter Radley (Treas); Back row: Doug Cunningham (Sect), Pete Driscoll, Jack Popowich, Bob Parent, Michel Blais, Mike Crombeen, Lloyd Aitken, Roger Dorey, Alex Forsyth, Gerry Wagar (V-P).

CHAPTER NINE

The Soaring Seventies

This decade saw the death of one brand of community hockey club and Kingston's step into the big leagues of junior hockey, with the importation of strange faces from across the province and even the United States. The 1970s belonged to Kingston Canadians, the city's first attempt at the highly publicized OHA Major Junior Hockey League that produces most of the NHL's stars.

Women's hockey came into its own with the formation of the Red Barons and championships attained by Queen's Golden Gals.

It was also a time when Kingston attracted professional team training camps, thanks to the aggressive attitude of Kingston's long-time Memorial Centre manager, Jim McCormick, and a link to a former Kingston product, which jumped to the big leagues.

The '70s also saw local boys—from the OMHA to the NHL—reach new heights. A few got their names inscribed on the game's most famous trophy.

The "Kingston" Bruins. The Limestone City has always had a close puck connection with The Hub — Boston. In fact, one writer tagged Kingston as "Boston North." In 1970, seven Kingston players attended the Bruins training camp: Front and centre: Fred O'Donnell and Hugh Harvey; Back row: Dick Cherry, Jim Adair, Wayne Cashman , Garry Young (scout), Rick Smith and Ron Plumb.

1971

THE MAJOR GOES BIG LEAGUE

Kingston peewees, coached by Dr. Gerry Wagar, won the prestigious North American Silver Stick championship in Port Huron, Michigan for their fifth tournament win. The team posted an amazing record of 50 wins, two losses and one tie and had four players—Ken Linseman, Rick Paterson, Rob Plumb and Mike Simurda—drafted later by NHL teams.

Long-time Kingston coach Major W.J. (Danny) McLeod was named the NHL's Supervisor of Officials, a position he held for eight years.

1972

YOUTH SETS EXAMPLE

Kingston's strong minor system paid double dividends this year when the minor bantams won the triple-A championship over Kitchener and the midget AAA all-stars triumphed over Windsor in three straight games. The young bantams eliminated Peterborough and Oshawa and whipped Don Maloney and his Kitchener mates three straight. In the final game Kenny Linseman scored five goals in an 8-4 victory for coach Brian Roe's club. The team was well-staffed with prospective juniors, including Bill Jenkins, Mike Simurda, Peter Young and Rick Coupland.

This was an age when Kingston minor all-star playoff teams drew crowds comparable to the seniors. The momentum for the midget stars built with victories over Peterborough, Oshawa and St. Catharines. Mike Babcock's boys, led by two-goal efforts of Dave Gollogly and Scott Ellis, drew 1,440 fans at Jock Harty in winning the OMHA title against Windsor. Seventeen hundred attended one of the Ontario final games against Sherry Bassin's Metro Toronto Hockey League winners, Wexford. For the fifth and deciding game, won by Wexford, there were 2,535 screaming supporters at the Memorial Centre. The RKMHA-picked team was well-balanced with Danny Marshall, George Patterson, Hal Pearson and Roger Dorey prominent on the attack.

The Aces, with ex-Junior A player Tom Thurlby as playing coach, were the top attraction in the city. With new recruits from Ted Walton's Junior B Frontenacs and veterans like Dick Cherry, Bob Olajos and Ron Earl, the Aces proved to be the power of the second division of the OHA Senior series, but fell to western teams in the playoffs. Kingston got a dose of NHL exposure this season as Garry Young, former Kingston minor hockey coach and now general manager of California Golden Seals, brought the expansion team to town. In a period of eight days, the Kingston Memorial Centre featured Pittsburgh Penguins, Minnesota North Stars, Philadelphia Flyers, Detroit Red Wings and

Dennis Kearns. This Kingston native enjoyed a solid 10-year NHL career with the Vancouver Canucks (1971-81), setting a team record for defenceman with 321 career points.

Ron Plumb. Shown with the Vancouver Blazers, Ron Plumb was named the WHA's best defenceman in 1977, the same honour he received in junior with the Peterborough Petes in 1970.

Syl Apps Jr. His father was a tough act to follow, but Syl Jr. played 10 NHL seasons and had a career high 99-point season with the Pittsburgh Penguins in 1975-76.

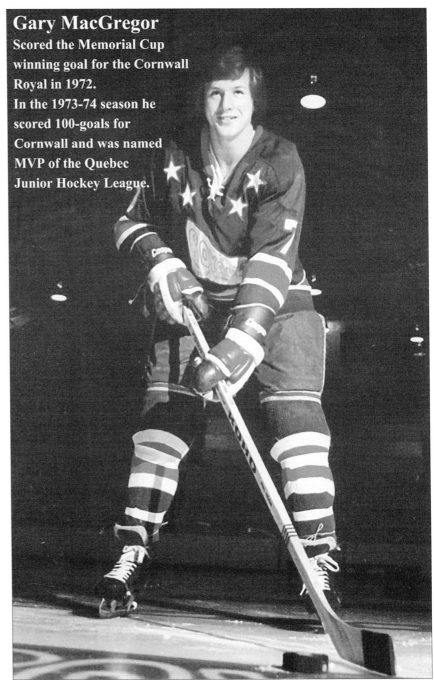

Gary MacGregor
Scored the Memorial Cup winning goal for the Cornwall Royal in 1972. In the 1973-74 season he scored 100-goals for Cornwall and was named MVP of the Quebec Junior Hockey League.

Bob Murray (top). The captain of the Memorial Cup champion Cornwall Royals, this stalwart defenceman played 15 years with the Chicago Blackhawks and had 514 career points.

Gord (Waldo) Wood (left). One of junior hockey's most respected scouts, he sent dozens of Kingston players on to junior and pro careers and won four Memorial Cup rings with Cornwall and Ottawa.

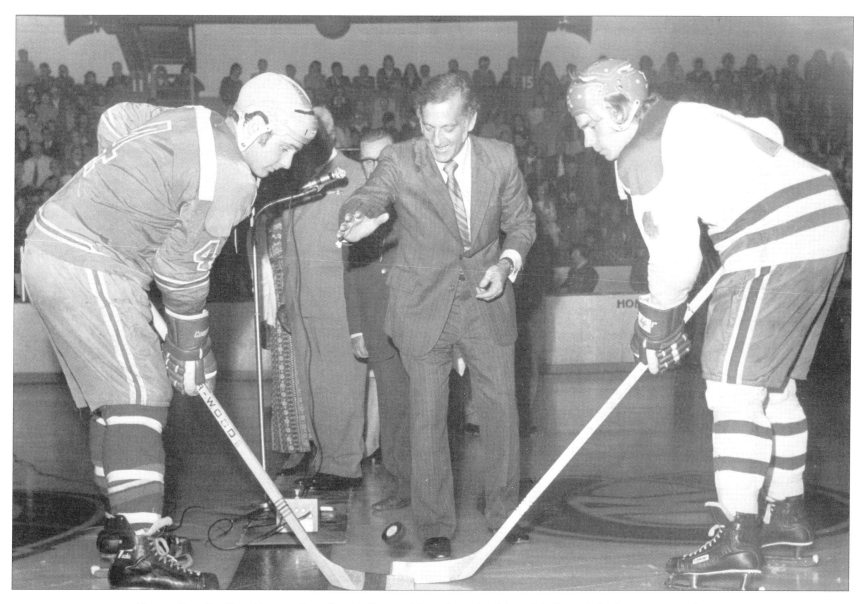

Kingston Canadians Franchise, 1973. A new franchise began as Mayor George Speal dropped the first puck for the Kingston Canadians'
debut in OHA Junior A competition against the Oshawa Generals. Kingston captain is Gord Buynak (right).

Buffalo Sabres. Two-thirds of the 3,343 seats were sold out for the first three games.

Kingston was very much a Boston Bruin town. And this year, one of the city's graduates on the Bean-town bruisers got his second drink of champagne from the Stanley Cup. Winger Wayne Cashman scored 23 goals for Boston and added four goals and seven assists in the playoffs to get his name on the cup for the second time.

In 1972, former Frontenac Harry Sinden coached Team Canada to a thrilling win against Soviet Russia in the Summit Series. Wayne Cashman played a key defensive role for Canada. Kingston's Gary MacGregor scored the winning goal as Cornwall Royals won the Memorial Cup. Captain of the Canadian champions was Kingston's Bob Murray, who would go on to a 15-year career with the Chicago Black Hawks.

1973

WELCOME JUNIOR A!

Kingston got its first taste of imported 20-years-and-under players when the Frontenacs entered the provincial Junior A league, a tier two loop. Coach Lorne Ferguson, a 13-year professional, was given a mixture of former Junior B's, Kingston midgets and talented juveniles and juniors from Pembroke, Listowel, Cornwall and Toronto and somehow survived a six-game losing streak to open the season.

With Jim Magee as club manager, the Junior Fronts provided a stepping-stone to tier one hockey.

On March 29, twelve Kingstonians, headed by the same James Magee, acquired the defunct Montreal Junior Canadiens franchise of the Ontario Major Junior Hockey League for $50,000. The first move was to sign Walter (Punch) Scherer, formerly of Kitchener Rangers, as general manager. He nabbed one of 13 Kingston and area players who were playing Junior A at the time, Roger Dorey, from London, and was blessed with some sharp draftees like midget Mike Crombeen, college player Greg Holst and rookie defenceman Mike O'Connell, who scored the team's first league goal.

Junior hockey meant improvements to the Memorial Centre. In midsummer, Jim McCormick and staff installed a plexiglas protective barrier around the ice surface in preparation for the inaugural season. It replaced the traditional wire screening.

Former Aces and RMC coach Danny McLeod, now a supervisor of officials for the NHL, was quoted as saying, "referees and linesmen are the only sane people at a hockey game."

Adding lustre to mid-season was Kingston's involvement in the first multi-nation hockey tournament. Teams from Finland, Sweden, Soviet Russia and Czechoslovakia met three OHA Senior A clubs. Played throughout Ontario, the round-

Mike O'Connell, Kingston Canadians 1973-75. The OHA's top defenceman in 1974-75, Mike O'Connell played 13 years in the NHL and is now the General Manager of the Boston Bruins.

Jay Wells, Kingston Canadians 1976-79. A rugged defenceman, he battled through 18 NHL seasons and played in more than 1,000 career games.

Tim Kerr, Kingston Canadians 1977-80. In a career cut short by injuries, Kerr was a 50-goal scorer four consecutive seasons for the Philadelphia Flyers (1984-87).

Mike Crombeen, Brad Rhiness and Tony McKegney, Kingston Canadians. These three Canadians stars combined for 947 career points in the 1970s.

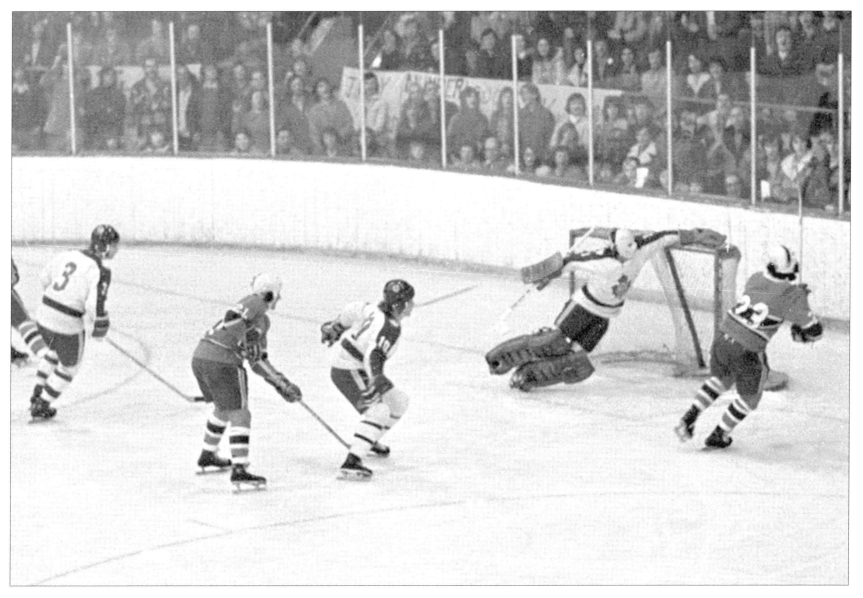

Playoff Fever. The Junior Canadians saw their first-ever playoff action in 1975, a thrilling eight-game series they lost to the Toronto Marlboros – the eventual Memorial Cup winners.

robin series was concluded in Kingston. Czecho-slovakia—with many national players—blasted the Aces, who featured four ex-pros and a future NHL star Bob Gainey. The closest a Canadian got to the trophy was Syl Apps, MLA for Kingston, who presented it to Czech captain Frank Pospisil.

The international influence had reached minor hockey in Canada. Kingston minor hockey all-stars, now entered in the Eastern Ontario district triple-A series, sent their best midgets up against Hammarby of Sweden and won 5-0.

Women's hockey garnered a headline when Queen's Golden Gals whipped the University of Toronto, 5-1, to capture the Ontario Women's Intercollegiate Athletic Association championship. Coached by Cookie Cartwright and led by the two-goal effort of Lesley Ferrari, and the goaltending of Wanda Gyde, the tricolour team won the title for the first time in 47 years.

Rugged defenceman Jim Dorey helped the New England Whalers win the WHA's first Avco Cup championship. He would win another cup with the Quebec Nordiques in 1977. Charlie Convery, the all-time leading scorer of the defunct Kingston Aces, moved on to play four more seasons with Belleville, Napanee and Whitby teams.

1974 THE VOYAGEURS ARRIVE

Five hockey die-hards, recognizing that the new Junior A Canadians would be made up almost entirely of imports, created a new hockey club—Kingston Township Voyageurs. Bruce Landon, Bill Darlington, Bill Reason, Jack Cliff and Bill Kay each threw $100 into the pot and the team entered the OHA Junior C series and played in the Kingston City League. Within a year, the all-volunteer organization had entered the Metro Junior B League against Belleville, Peterborough, Oshawa and Toronto area teams, and were faced with an annual budget of almost $20,000.

The California Seals were back in Kingston in the fall with a series of pre-season exhibition games against NHL clubs. With expansion continuing and line-ups diluted, the bloom was off for professional teams in small towns. Atlanta Flames drew only 662 fans. There were only 393 paid admissions for a game three nights later with New York Islanders. However, Kingstonians were still enamoured with members of the so-called "Original Six" as Chicago Black Hawks attracted 2,908 in going down to the Seals 4-2.

The Canadians, in their first season, proved very competitive. They won 20 games and finished 10 points ahead of last-place Hamilton. Nearly every $2.50 and $2 seat was filled every game, and

Kingston Rotary-Kiwanis OMHA Minor Bantam AAA Champions, 1971-72. Front row: Roddy Todd, Brian Clancy, Mike Simurda, Rick Paterson, Ken Linseman, Bob Moses, Rick Coupland; Second row: Ron Brown (Manager), Neil Faulkner, Mike Ignas, Steve Wilson, Bill Jenkins, Steve Young, Tim Torrance, John Gurnsey, Brian Roe (Coach); Insets: Mark Jackson, Cam MacGregor. Ken "Baby Bull" Linseman was drafted by the WHA Birmingham Bulls six years later.

standing room went for one buck. The directors paid off their investment midway through the season. Jack (Red) Bownass, with 13 years as a pro player and two as a coach in Sweden, was elected the league's coach of the year.

One Kingston-developed player who got away was Gary MacGregor. The son of former senior star Gary MacGregor scored 100 goals and passed for 74 others to help lead Cornwall Royals to first place in the west group of the Quebec Major Junior Hockey League. Second and third in team scoring were two other Kingstonians, Kevin Treacy, 156 points, and defenceman Bob Murray, 99 points. Bob Ferguson and Terry Angel rounded out the Kingston contingent recruited by Gordie (Waldo) Woods.

A group of 16-and-under players stole the spotlight this season. Kingston Gurnsey Midgets, coached and managed by Gerry Wagar and Jimmy Hare, qualified for the national Wrigley tournament. Sparked by Ken Linseman, with 13 goals and six assists, the Kingston kids won four out of five first-round matches. In the final, they outshot the undefeated Quebec club 44-17 but lost 5-3. The disappointed losers never regained their winning style and lost in the OMHA provincial playdowns. Linseman, who won the most valuable player award and a $1,000 educational scholarship, was headed for stardom with another Kingston club.

Ex-Kingston Ace Dave Gilmour had his best year in the pros with 34 goals and 31 assists for Baltimore of the AHL.

Lorne D. Cook, who dedicated most of his life to the game and was named a life member of the OHA in 1972, died. A trophy in his name was donated and awarded to the Kingston Canadians top rookie.

Rick Smith played for the WHA team Canada all-stars against the Soviet Union in an eight-game series in Canada and Russia.

1975

CANADIANS SONT LA!

Deft drafting helped the Canadians earn the title of Cinderella team in Kingston's second season in the Major Junior A loop. Two Mikes led the way: Mike O'Connell was named the league's most valuable defenceman and Mike Crombeen led the team in scoring with 115 points. Tony McKegney showed signs of greatness, but it was the play of Kingstonians Ken Linseman, Roger Dorey, Larry Murphy, Bob Parent and Rob Plumb that added spice for the fans. Brad Rhiness set a league record with three goals in 28 seconds against Windsor. Punch Scherer took over as coach with four games left in the regular season and the Canadians almost pulled off the upset of the year against George Armstrong's Toronto Marlboros, the eventual Memorial Cup champions, before losing in eight games.

Ken Linseman, Wrigley Cup MVP. He graduated to the Kingston Canadians and, as an underage junior, turned pro with the WHA's Birmingham Bulls in 1977-78, where he had 38-goals and 76-points in his only WHA season.

Kingston Gurnsey Midgets, Wrigley Cup Midget Finalists, 1974. Coached by Dr. Gerry Wagar, this team dropped a 5-3 decision to Quebec in the championship game at the Wrigley Cup Canadian Midget Hockey Championships.

Kingston Township Voyageurs, 1976-77. The Ontario Metro Junior B Hockey League arrived in Kingston in the 1970s with the Kingston Township Voyageurs. The Vees have sent many players on to the NHL, OHL and US Colleges, including Scott Arniel, Kirk Muller, Rik Wilson and Alyn McCauley. Front row: Tim Anderson, David Ottenhoff, Dick Cherry (Coach), Tom Thurlby (Asst Coach), Mike Dawson (Capt), Paul Hoag (GM), Lloyd Babcock (Pres), Larry Murphy, Rick Coupland; Middle Row: Paul Watts (Stats), Tim McKeown, Reg Walton, John Morrison, Kevin Scott, Steve Arniel, Ron Folk, Bert Vonhertzberg (Trainer). Back Row: Terry Kelly, Joe Scherer, Jamie McLelland, Dan Hobbs, Steve Cherry, Kevin Sands, John Linseman; Missing: Neil Faulkner.

Wayne Gretzky, April 1972. Only 11 years old and wearing No. 9, the 'Great One' led his Brantford Steelers to victory before a packed Constantine Rink. The superstar to-be scored 17 goals during the tournament to reach 700 for the season. In this Whig-Standard *photo he duels with Kingston Young Nats' Bob Earle.*

Another crimson-sweatered team attracted attention this season. The Red Barons, organized five years ago, established themselves as the No. 1 senior women's team in Ontario. Star amateur golfer Katherine (Cookie) Cartwright was the catalyst for the team, along with Annabelle Twiddy, who sparkled on the wing. The "Kid Line" featured daughters of three men with extensive hockey backgrounds: Jeanie Gerow, now Janean Sergeant (Napanee Comets coach Walt Gerow), Sue Scherer (Kingston Canadians GM Punch Scherer) and Kim Ferguson (Ex-NHLer Lorne Ferguson). Ferguson went on to Queen's and a selection as the outstanding woman college player, while Scherer starred for Canada's world champions in 1990. Solid on defence for coach Bob Weatherdon's team were hard-shooting Sue Wright and Rhonda Leeman, who carved out a career as developmental co-ordinator for the Ontario Women's Hockey Association in the early 1980s.

In minor hockey, a Kingston youth was being compared with a recent goal-scoring sensation from Brantford, Wayne Gretzky. Nine-year-old Kirk Muller scored an amazing 213 goals for Central City Auto Parts novices.

The hockey community was saddened by the death of Harold Harvey, 76, founder of the Church Athletic League at Kingston General Hospital.

Syl Apps, Jr., who enjoyed a point-a-game sea-son with the Pittsburgh Penguins, was selected for the NHL all-star game and named the most valuable player.

1976 — JIMMY STARTS HIS REIGN

Jim Morrison, an 11-year NHL veteran and former mentor of Baltimore's World Hockey Association team, took over the coaching reigns and the Kingston Canadians never looked back.

The most exciting player for the Canadians was hometowner Ken Linseman. The pesky centreman, just 17 years of age, scored a hat trick in Sudbury to reach the 50-goal plateau. He finished the year with a team-record 61 goals and 51 assists for 112 points.

Kingston fans had another local boy to marvel over. Gary MacGregor scored 44 goals and earned 34 assists for Chicago Cougars of the WHA and lost the rookie of the year award to experienced Swedish star Anders Hedberg.

A son of the late Kingston Goodyears' star, George MacGregor, Gary drew rave notices this season with the Denver Spurs of the same league. "He's a great one—a really smart, very fast centre," manager-coach Jean-Guy Talbot told Toronto writer Dan Proudfoot. "He can be a superstar."

Jim Morrison. Kingston Canadians enjoyed some of their finest years with Jim Morrison behind the bench (1975-1982).

Len Coyle. As the Canadians' Assistant Trainer, Len has been with Kingston's junior franchise since day one in 1973. Sharpening skates and keeping equipment in order, the genial gent is still at it — with a smile and a quip.

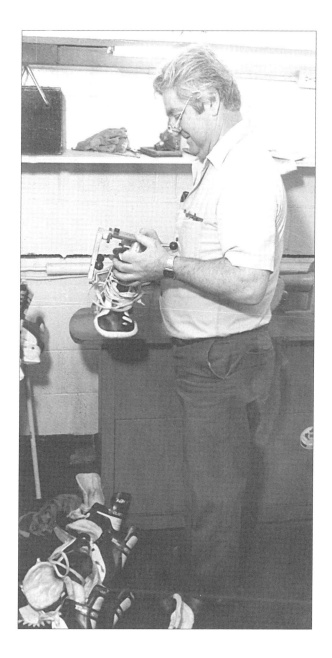

Walter 'Punch" Scherer. The first General Manager of the Canadians.

1977 WHA DRAFTS KENNY

Exceptionally well coached by Wayne Kirk and his assistant Morris Kelso fifteen 11-year-olds from Kingston Township stole the limelight this year by winning the OMHA Minor Pee Wee AA title.

The Canadians jumped to third place on 32 wins and 10 ties and lost to Ottawa 67s in the Leyden division final. In a bitterly fought series, Ken Linseman was suspended from the play-offs for kicking Ottawa defenceman Jeff Geiger during a fight. Linseman scored 53 goals in 63 games and assisted on 74 others. He finished fifth in the league in scoring, eight points behind all-star left winger Tony McKegney, who compiled 58 goals—23 on the power play—and 77 assists. The penalty minutes of the truculent Linseman, however, topped his total points 210 to 127. In June, he was selected as an underage junior by Birmingham Bulls of the World Hockey Association.

In 1977, Kingston Canadian grad Alex Forsyth, a first round draft choice of the Washington Capitals, played his only NHL game. Ron Plumb of the Cincinnati Stingers was named the WHA's best defenceman after a 69-point season. Dennis Kearns of the Vancouver Canucks played for Team Canada at both the 1977 and 1978 World Hockey Championships.

1978 FASTEST SKATER

Tony McKegney (43-49-92 in 55 games) was chosen "fastest skater" in the major junior league, but the rest of the Canadians added up to a fourth-place finish. Speedy underage defenceman Paul Coffey was a late season call-up from the North York Rangers and recorded two goals and two assists in eight games for the Canadians.

International hockey returned to Kingston in mid-season with a Finland team meeting The Entertainer, Eddie Shack, and the Pop Shoppe Pops in an entertaining exhibition.

In the WHA, a 38-38 goals-assists record with the Birmingham Bulls earned Ken Linseman a seventh-place overall draft by the NHL Philadelphia Flyers. Behn Wilson went sixth to the same team. In the NHL, Don Cherry of the Boston Bruins won the Jack Adams Award as the Coach of the Year.

1979 DOC'S LADS DO IT

Kingston Canadians' 26 wins were good enough for fifth place, thanks to defenceman Jay Wells and goalkeeper Avelino Gomez, a pair of division all-stars.

Ken Linseman started the season with the AHL Maine Mariners and garnered 40 points in 38 games to earn a promotion to Philadelphia. With the Flyers, he potted only five goals but passed for 20 others in 30 games.

Ernestown OMHA Midget B Champions, 1978-79. Front row: Greg Anderson, Greg Latham, Scott Rawding, Joe Proderick, Jamie Carty; Middle row: Mike White (Coach), Bob Landon (Coach), David Leder, Steve Burtch, Steve Leonard, Kevin Wolfram, Bill Godkin (Mgr), Bill Murray (Sponsor). Back row; Pete Giddy, Dan Dirocco, Dan Allen, Joe O'Connor, Trevor Tackaberry, Steve Franklin.

Lakeview Manor Oldtimers. One of the over-35 clubs playing in oldtimers' leagues in the 1970s. Front row: Bill Hudson, Eddie Watts, Bill Carr, Denis Armacher, Eric Elmquist, Ronald Ouimet, Joe Corcoran; Back row: Bill Hamilton, Bob Johnston, Bill Depew, Wallace Toby Sudds, Hughy McDonald, Jim Woods, Tom Loftus, John O'Connor; Absent, Wayne Sudds, Bob Bryant, Louis Lessard.

The Voyageurs reached into the Kingston Township Minor Hockey Association for a new coach to succeed Dick Cherry. Wayne Kirk, Head of Civil Engineering at RMC, led the team to a second-place finish and was named Coach of the Year in the OHA Metro Junior B league. The V's lost out in six games to Mike Keenan's Oshawa Legionnaires led by Dale Hawerchuk.

Captain Tim Huleatt, second to 30-goal scorer Scott Arniel, was awarded the Terry Kelly Memorial Trophy, presented in memory of Terry who played for the Vees in 1976-78 and was killed in a bicycle accident the previous year. Rik Wilson was chosen most valuable defenceman and Ted Linseman was named most gentlemanly player.

Condie Pontiac all-stars topped the highly competitive Eastern Ontario Major Midget AAA league with 14 wins in 19 games. Coached by Dr. Gerry Wagar, the team lost two players, who inadvertently signed Junior B cards, and lost the playoffs against Peterborough. Marty Stover was the top scorer and a lad named Doug Gilmour was an offensive defenceman.

In the NHL, tough Kingston defenceman Jay Wells was a first round draft pick of the L.A. Kings and went on to an 18-year career of 1,000 plus NHL games. A too-many-men-on-the-ice penalty in a Stanley Cup play-off game in Montreal spelled the end of Don Cherry's coaching career in Boston, where he had guided the Bruins to four consecutive division titles. After a year coaching Colorado Rockies, he joined CBC's *Hockey Night in Canada*.

JUNIOR A LOSES ITS LUSTRE

In his first full season in the NHL, Ken Linseman, unaffectionately known as "The Rat," put together respectable 22-57 goals-assists numbers in 80 games for Philadelphia and held his penalty minutes to 107. In the playoffs, he led all others with 18 assists and also tallied four goals for the Flyers.

The decade ended with hope as Jim Morrison's Canadians won 35 games and clinched fourth place in the Leyden division. An unrecognized diamond in the rough was rangy Tim Kerr, who potted 40 goals and added 33 assists, almost doubling his previous year's production.

Syl Apps, Jr., who played his last amateur hockey for Kingston Aces and Junior Frontenacs, wound up a ten-year career in the NHL with 806 points, but fewer goals than his illustrious father in pre-expansion days. Rick Smith was in his 11th and last season in the NHL.

The Church Athletic League celebrated its 30th anniversary with a record of 50,000 boys and girls on 112 teams from 63 parishes meeting church and Sunday school attendance requirements.

Three Kingston Canadian defencemen were among the top 25 picks at the NHL draft: Rik Wilson (St. Louis/12th overall), Mike Stothers (Philadelphia/21st) and Craig Muni (Toronto/25th).

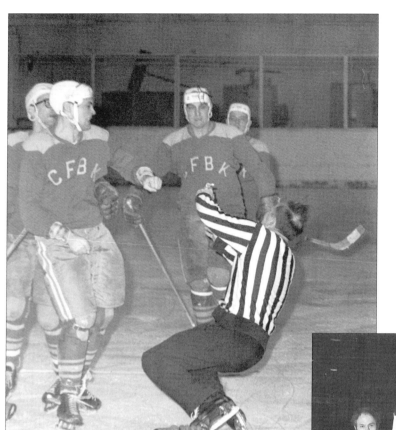

Hockey Violence. In this remarkable 1970s shot by Kingston photographer Bob Johnston, a CFB Kingston player decks the referee with a stiff left hook. The official broke his ankle in the skirmish and the anonymous player was suspended.

Kingston Condie Pontiac Midget All-Stars, 1977-78. Dr. Gerry Wagar and Richard (Wink) Wilson developed many minor hockey players who went on to junior and pro careers. Ten players from this team were drafted into the OHL and two went on to NHL careers: Rik Wilson and Scott Arniel. Front row: Rob Castelvetri, Mike Thompson, Mike Deodato (Capt), Rik Wilson, Brian Abrams; Middle row: Gerry Wagar (Coach), Steve Murphy, Todd Muller, Marty Stover, Dennis Pennock, Maurice Godin, Ian MacInnis, Richard 'Wink' Wilson (GM/Asst Coach); Back row: Gary Kremsater, Rob Joyce, Dusty Street, Scott Arniel, Jim Callaghan, Bruce Marchant.

The *Kingston* Hockey Centennial

The Puck Is Dropped

SOME DAY, A DIVER IN the Flora MacDonald Confederation Park Basin in front of Centennial Park at City Hall will discover a handful of odd-shaped rubber missiles. These unique pucks were shot from the shore onto thin ice by VIPs and hockey buffs using historic hockey sticks on January 1, 1986. The rare event kicked off one of the longest celebrations in the city's history—the Kingston Hockey Centennial (KHC). Sponsored by the International Hockey Hall of Fame and Museum, the year-long series of celebrations was directed by Bill Hamilton, a not-so-old-time hockey player and financed by the sale of 10,324 Hockey Centennial Dollars.

A few yards away, in warmer weather, the KHC erected a granite bench marking the first hockey game played on that Kingston harbour site between Queen's and RMC. Kingston Canadians wore a special 1886-1986 patch showing the blade of the historic hockey stick and square puck used in that history-making game.

To help celebrate the occasion, Maurice (The Rocket) Richard came to town for No. 9 Night at Legion No. 9 and joined Jo-Jo Graboski in saluting Kingston's hockey heritage and the Major Junior A Canadians. The KHC committee sponsored a suc-

cessful art show, *The Canadian Game*, a first of its kind in Canada. Including more than 100 fine art paintings and illustrations, the show was curated by Kingston artist and hockey fan Joan Belch. She also created *Lenny,* a bronze sculpture of the player, Lennox Irving who scored the first goal in the first Kingston game. The nine-inch high figure became part of the Carr-Harris Cup trophy that was awarded to the winner of the first Causeway Challenge Series between RMC and Queen's.

The Kingston hockey story was broadcast nation-wide when CBC's *Fresh Air* show presented a public breakfast program from Howard Johnson Hotel overlooking the site of the first game. Hosts Bill McNeil and Cy Strange reminisced with two Hall of Famers, the Cook brothers, Bill and Bun, who spread Kingston's name throughout North America with their dazzling passing and scoring plays for the New York Rangers in the 1920s and 1930s.

The year was concluded with a rousing celebration at 401 Inn featuring Kingston's most famous hockey personality, Don Cherry. The colourful *Hockey Night in Canada* commentator was one of 52 recipients of Kingston 100 Award certificates "in recognition of having made an outstanding contribution to the development and promotion of the game of hockey in Kingston."

"These are the people who know hockey," said Cherry, the KHS honourary chairman. "When I'm on television, these are the people I'm talking to."

For the record, the Kingston 100 Award recipients were: Harry Acton, Bud Aitken, Cookie Cartwright, Art Casterton, Don Cherry, Dick Cherry, Jack Cliff, Charlie Convery, Len Coyle, Don Crawford, Leon Doucet, Cliff Earl, Bill Farrar, Lorne Ferguson, Ruth Fisher, Bernard Fleming, Alec Gaudreau, Don Goodridge, Ken Goodridge, Don Gilmour, Fred Gurnsey, Pat Hegarty, Max Jackson, Hank Kelly, Bill Kirkpatrick, Gary Lavallee, Ken Linseman,

Don L'Oiseau, Reg Locke, Bob Londry, Jim Magee, Gus Marker, Phil Marshall, Scotty Martin, Don Murray, Danny McLeod, George MacGregor, Wayne Nichols, Ken Partis, Ed Plumb, Jerry Polywakan, Bill Reason, Ken Reid, Ron Robinson, Brian Roe, Don Senior, Gerry Wagar, Ted Walton, Gwen Walker, Clair Williamson, Gord Wood and Garry Young. Kingston has so man worthy hockey people that 48 others could well have been honoured to make it an even 100.

By special request "Grapes" read a poem extolling referees and then heard one, *The Puck is Dropped,* written and presented by Kingston's Poet of the People, James Michael Chapeskie.

THE PUCK IS DROPPED
(A poem written for the celebration of 100 years of hockey in Kingston).

In Kingston
We hold jubilee.
Old memories
Gleam forth again.
History revolves
Her divergent wings
And in their silver we see
Golden smiles
As hockey players
Skate on the harbour
In the wind.

The illustrious historical
Achievements
That we share this year

With fellow Canadians
And the world
I parallel
With the delights themselves
Of swirling skates
And whirling sticks,
To the sharp trilling sound
Of steel on ice,
To the bluster and paint
Of resilient crackle
And clicking
To the dogged tenacity
To win or die hard.

Square Puck. The most popular souvenir among collectors was this replica of the puck used in the first game on the harbour ice in 1886. Five thousand of the discs were produced for the Kingston shrine by the late Phil Quattrocchi.

Maurice (Rocket) Richard Ribbon. The Rocket was honoured at 'Number 9 Night' at No. 9 Legion during the Kingston Hockey Centennial celebrations in 1986. All guests, including Kingston Canadians, received red and white commemorative ribbons.

The strategic and tactical
Forethought,
The mental concentration
Entangled in the hum
Of the vision of the prize,
The uneasiness,
The despondency
The glimmer of hope,
The quickness of timing
To shoot to score,
The technically masterful
Attack and defence
And facial expressions
Of lunge
Read wit
And keep at bay,
The unflagging sweat,
The dynamic spirit
And tumult full of life
All which impel
Pull and eddy
The spectator's hearts
Into prompt, melodious applause
Or hurl them ardently
Into giddy tremors
At the spiral motion
Of the puck
Or the whirlwind rush
Of players.
The fluctuating intrigue
Of a game of hockey

Symbolizeth like human history
Something above
And beyond itself –
Perhaps the very powers
Of life and mind –
Perhaps the struggles
Of temporal civilizations –
Perhaps the complexity
Of interpreting the last victory
Of survival
Under such problematic conditions
Of all that is most dear
And precious to us. . .

The cold ice
So warmly intimate
Like tonight the stars
Of heaven were;
The dream of those
Who watch
That their team might win;
Opposing glances
Insignias,
Colours;
A harmonious hush,
A hopeful, cheerful readiness;
Quicken'd pulses –
A magnificent moment
And the puck is dropped!

— James Michael Chapeskie

Kingston, Ontario, 1986

"Lenny." A sculpture designed by Kingston's Joan Belch commemorated Lennox Irving, who scored the only goal in the first game between Queen's and RMC in 1886. The sculpture became part of the Carr-Harris Cup trophy.

CHAPTER TEN

The Exasperating Eighties

Hockey went on a roller coaster ride in the 1980s, with more downs than ups, unfortunately. The junior hockey club, the longest-running franchise in the city hit a desperate, dark low and then a short-lived but bright high under new ownership.

Except for Queen's varsity squad, the decade passed without one Kingston team winning a major provincial championship, but the minor hockey "star wars" ended with amalgamation. In the late '80s, fans had to look to the township minors, regional women's teams and the Junior B Voyageurs for special achievements.

Players, fans and officials took time out to celebrate the 100th anniversary of the game in Kingston with a series of public events. One was the reinvigoration of hockey's oldest rivalry, Queen's vs. RMC, with the establishment of the "Causeway Challenge Series" for a cup celebrating the contribution of the Carr-Harris family to both institutions and to hockey.

And Kingstonians continued to cast their puck-trained eyes to television and newspapers to follow the locals in their pro careers. One "Limestoner" reached the pinnacle with a salute from Lord Stanley.

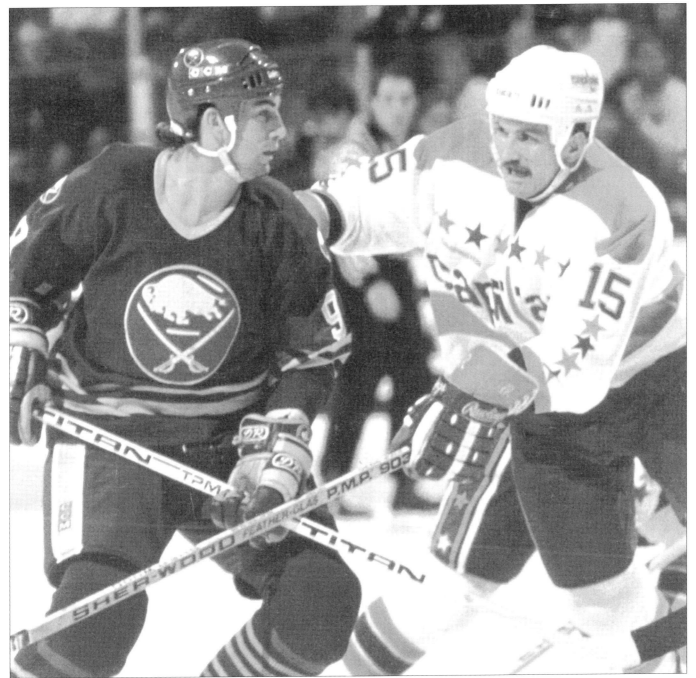

Scott Arniel. After winning two Memorial Cups with the Cornwall Royals and a World Junior Championship for Canada in 1982, Scott Arniel became a solid two-way player during 11 NHL seasons and is now an assistant coach with the Buffalo Sabres.

Major W.J. (Danny) McLeod. Supervisor of officials in the NHL for 10 years and former director of athletics at RMC, Major McLeod had previously served as a coach of Kingston junior, senior and intercollegiate hockey teams.

Art Casterton. The only Kingston-born official to referee in the National Hockey League, Art Casterton (right) was named to the OHA's Honour Roll in 1982 for 25 years of service.

NHL Entry Draft, June 9, 1984. Kirk Muller, Mario Lemieux and Eddie Olczyk celebrate their top selections at the NHL entry draft. Muller was selected second overall by New Jersey.

Kirk Muller. This Kingston boy began his OHL career as a 15-year-old underage player with the Kingston Canadians in the 1981-82 season, collecting 51-points.

1981

BERNIE LEADS CANADIANS

The Canadians, sparked by crafty Bernie Nicholls, won a franchise-high 39 games, finished third in the Leyden Division but lost in the division final to Sault Ste. Marie. Nicholls fired 61 goals to top Linseman's previous club record of 56 and set a total-points mark of 152. Rik Wilson set a scoring record for Kingston defencemen with a 100-point season. Scott Howson made the most of his final junior year by scoring 57 goals, collecting 140 points and adding 19 points in the playoffs.

Dennis Kearns, a graduate of Rotary-Kiwanis Minor Hockey Association and Kingston Aces, wound up a 10-year NHL career with Vancouver Canucks. A strong point player, he earned 31 goals and 290 assists in 677 games.

Kingston lost one of its unique sporting characters when George Joseph (Joe) King (whose personal cards read "JOKING") died, aged 84. A native of Toronto, where he started his 50-year career in baseball and hockey promotion, the bow-tied hustler published the first illustrated history of hockey, which sold for $2 in 1923. A super ad salesman, Joe moved to Kingston, published numerous hockey programs, supported lacrosse and served as president and drumbeater for city senior hockey leagues until his last days.

Elsewhere in the OHA, rookie Doug Gilmour, a Kingston boy, scored the winning goal as the Cornwall Royals win their second straight Memorial Cup title. Teammate Scott Arniel, another Kingston grad recruited by Kingstonian Gordon (Waldo) Wood, played on both Canadian championship teams.

Former Boston Bruin Fred O'Donnell was nominated for national university coaching honours after the Queen's Golden Gaels tied Toronto for first place in the intercollegiate league and went on to the Canadian finals in Calgary. It was the Kingston university's first Ontario intercollegiate title in 65 years. "It was a pretty good character team," recalled the man who was behind the Gaels' bench for eight seasons. The Gaels had the sensational goaltending of Andy Chisholm and the scoring talent of Paul Stothart (63 goals)—and the support of Ron Davidson, Don Folk and Steve Cherry.

1982

CANADIANS IN DECLINE

After struggling from last to third place, the Canadians started a long decline by playing .500 hockey and slipping to fifth in the re-named Ontario Hockey League under coach and GM Jim Morrison. Mike Siltala led the Kingston Canadians in scoring (36-44-80) after 51 games. The poor finish brought an end to Jim Morrison's seven-year career as coach and GM of the Canadians. He was

Bernie Nicholls, Kingston Canadians, 1979-81 (above). As an NHL player, Bernie scored 475 NHL goals during an 18-year career, including a 70-goal season for the L.A. Kings in 1988-89.

Rik Wilson, Kingston Canadians 1979-81 (right). St. Louis Blues 1st round draft choice in 1980, Rik is the only Kingston defenceman to record a 100-point season in the OHL with the Kingston Canadians in 1980-81.

replaced by Rod Graham, who lasted one season.

Junior playing days ended for Kingston's Rik Wilson. A three-year key member of the Canadians' defence corps and a St. Louis Blues' first round draft choice, Wilson made it in the NHL.

Ted Walton's Greenwood Oldtimers won the C division title at the World Oldtimers Hockey Championships in Toronto. The Kingston line-up included former Aces' stars Ron Earl, Charlie Convery, Rod Graham and Dick Cherry, plus Doug Cunningham, a co-owner of the Kingston Canadians.

Art Casternon is named to the OHA's Honour Roll for 25 years of service as a referee. He is one of only ten men to receive the provincial honour.

Canadian goaltender Mike Moffat backstopped Canada to a gold medal win at the World Junior Hockey Championships in Minnesota and played outstandingly for Boston in the NHL playoffs. Scott Arniel, who played on Canada's gold medal winning team, was drafted by the Winnipeg Jets, their 2nd pick.

High on the bestseller list in Kingston was *Grapes—A Vintage View of Hockey* by "dapper, loquacious" Don Cherry. As told to New York writer Stan Fischler, this autobiography featured a revealing chapter: "Early Life in Kingston."

1983

THREE 50 GOAL SCORERS

The Kingston Canadians had three 50-goal scorers—Ron Handy, Keith Knight and Mike Siltala—and still managed to miss the playoffs in the Leyden division. Handy had 52 goals and 148 points to finish second in league scoring behind Doug Gilmour of the Cornwall Royals. Gilmour's total of 177 was the third highest garnered in league history, behind only Ottawa's Bobby Smith and Sault Ste. Marie's Wayne Gretzky. Gilmour set a record 55-game point scoring streak and was chosen as the league's all-star centre. Doug's linemate, another Kingston native, Ian MacInnis, fired 59 goals and earned 133 assists. "Gilly" was named the OHL's most outstanding player. Yet another grad of the Kingston minor hockey system, Kirk Muller, was judged Ontario's most gentlemanly player while playing for the Guelph Platers.

Kingston's tradition of producing good players and developing fine coaches—from Ray Marchand to Don Blackburn and Don Cherry—was exemplified this year in women's hockey. Rhonda Leeman, who starred for Queen's Golden Gals, became coach of York Yeowomen. For the past four seasons she had been development co-ordinator for the Ontario Women's Hockey Association.

In 1983, Harry Sinden, who played and worked in Kingston, before becoming coach and general

Queen's Golden Gaels, O.U.A.A. Champions, 1980-81. Coached by former Boston Bruin Fred O'Donnell, this team became the most successful Queen's hockey club in the modern era. Front row: Andy Chishold, Dr. Murray Mitchell, Ron Davidson, Glenn Surbey (Asst Coach), John McIntyre, Fred O'Donnell (Coach), Paul Stothart, Dr. Fraser Saunders, John Lloyd; Middle row: Al Allmark (trainer), Tom Powers, Ross Moffat, Joe South, Dean Anastas, Mike Skube, Joe Minken, Dave Farris, Julian Lewis (Manager), Al Kellar; Back row: Rich Minken, John Nightingale, Mike Kruse, Ron Strike, John Murray, Steve Cherry, Ron Folk, Al McKee, Steve Watt.

manager of the Boston Bruins, was inducted into the Hockey Hall of Fame. Wayne Cashman retired after a 17-year, 1,222 game, 298 goal, 871 point career with the Boston Bruins. He was the last "Original Six" player to retire.

1984

SEVEN IS UNLUCKY

The Ken Slater-Rick Cornacchia duo was in charge of managing and coaching the Canadians, but the results were an unlucky "7"—seventh in the Leyden. However, there were a few bright spots. Tim Salmon became the Canadian's first league scoring champion, winning the 1983-84 OHL scoring title with 45 goals and 145 points. Linemate Kevin Conway led the league with 65 goals, collected 130 points and was named the league's most gentlemanly player. Six of his goals came in a one-game rampage against Belleville.

In the NHL, Ken Linesman scored the winning goal as the Edmonton Oilers knocked off the four-time champion New York Islanders to win their first of five Stanley Cups in a seven-year span.

Eighteen-year-old Kirk Muller, the second pick overall in the NHL draft, became the youngest player to compete for Canada in Olympic hockey. Trevor Stienburg from nearby Moscow, Ontario, Muller's former teammate, was taken 15th overall by Quebec Nordiques.

1985

THE LINSEMEN BROTHERS' ACT

Kingston's OHL team fell from 25 wins in 1984 to 18 but hung on to seventh place. Fans had little to cheer about other than Scott Metcalfe's 60-point season and Ted Linseman's 13 goals and 27 assists. Linseman's brother, Steve, scored 57 goals and tallied 140 points for the Belleville Bulls. Three other brothers—Ken, John and Mike—played in Ontario's premier junior league.

Former NHL and WHA player Fred O'Donnell, after an eight-year career behind the bench of the Queen's Golden Gaels, was signed as coach and general manager of the Kingston Canadians. With Kingston's Marty Abrams in goal, the Sault Ste. Marie Greyhounds went through the entire 66-game season undefeated on home ice and advanced to the Memorial Cup. Kingston native Tim Ferguson, in his final OHL season, scored 46 goals and recorded 101 points for the Cornwall Royals.

Kingston's forgotten academic team, the St. Lawrence Vikings, won the OCAA hockey championship under the direction of coach Ron Robinson.

Off ice the biggest hockey happening was the appearance of NHL President John Ziegler. He spoke at a testimonial dinner for Hall of Famer Syl Apps and his late wife, Molly, but was upstaged by Don (Grapes) Cherry. Grapes, in describing the peerless Toronto Maple Leaf great, "If you looked

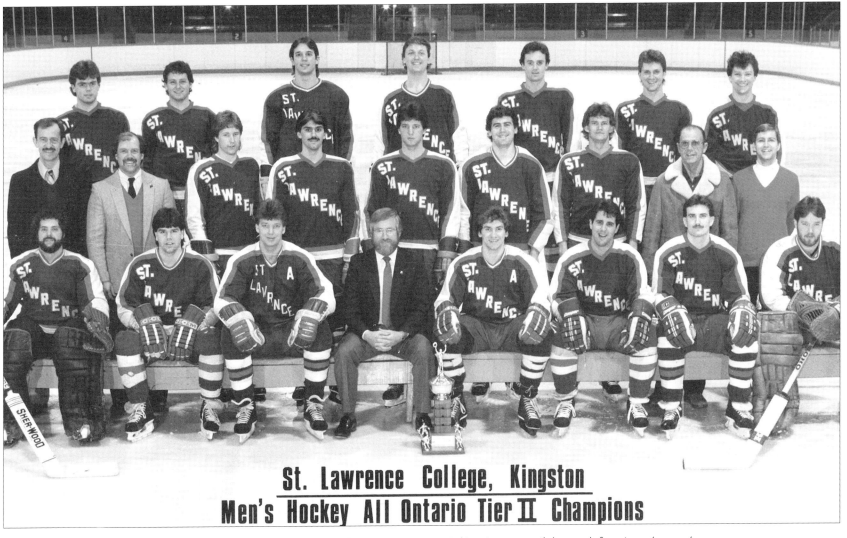

St. Lawrence College, Kingston
Men's Hockey All Ontario Tier II Champions

St. Lawrence College Vikings, O.C.A.A. Tier II Champions, 1984-85. Ron Robinson's team compiled a record of 50-wins, 15-losses and 5-ties. Front row: Butch LaPorte, Derrick Dupuis, Dan Hobbs, Ron Robinson, (Coach), Jim Whelan, Joe MacInnis, Darrell MacKay, David Smith; Second row: Brian Hobbin, (Asst Coach), Paul Hannah (Asst Coach), John Lawrence, Lee Sheets, Todd Hobbs, John Blackburn, Ken Sizer, George McMillan (Manager) Doug Allsebrook (Stats); Back row: Chris Rioux, Jeff Forbes, Paul Dickey, David Bowley, Dan Coffey, Bob Van Niedek, Pat Iselmoe.

up the word 'gentleman' [in a dictionary] your picture would be there."

In 1985, Kirk Muller, representing New Jersey, made his first of six appearances in the NHL all-star game.

1986

HE SHOOTS, HE SCORES!

The Canadians, wearing "Kingston Hockey Centennial 1886-1986" shoulder patches, responded to their new mentor with nearly double the number of wins (35) over the previous season and finished fourth in the Leyden—their best mark in five years. Brian Verbeek led the offence with 50 goals and 40 assists. Kingston goaltender Chris Clifford gains national attention as the first goaltender in the Canadian Major Junior hockey to score a goal. He fired the puck the length of the ice into an open net during a game against Toronto Marlboros at the Kingston Memorial Centre.

One hundred years of hockey in Kingston was celebrated with numerous special events, including the Historic Hockey series, No. 9 Night with Maurice Richard, a hockey art exhibition and the Kingston 100 Award, in which Don Cherry passed out certificates to many players, coaches and officials.

The Carr-Harris Cup series, celebrating the 100-year-old rivalry between RMC and Queen's, was inaugurated as part of the Centennial celebrations. RMC surprised Ron Plumb's Gaels 8-3.

The first step in ending disagreements in minor hockey in Kingston was launched when a committee was appointed to look into the amalgamation of city, township, CAL and Ernestown Township organizations into a Greater Kingston association.

1987

PEACE IN THE MINORS

Under the leadership of Kingston's Leon Doucet, the Greater Kingston Minor Hockey Association was formed with co-operation of the Kingston Minor Hockey Association, the Kingston Township Minor Hockey Association and the Church Athletic League. The region was represented by the best players on "rep" teams at all levels of AAA competition.

RMC forward Steve Molaski, with 195 lifetime points, moved into sixth place on the OUAA's career hockey scoring list. One notch above is Queen's golden Gaels' winger Paul Stothart at 204 points.

In just his fourth NHL season, 21-year-old Kirk Muller was named captain of the New Jersey Devils.

Tim Salmon, Kingston Canadians. The only Kingston Canadians player to win the OHL scoring championship, Tim topped the league scoring race in 1983-84 with 45-goals and 145-points.

Chris Clifford Scores! Kingston Canadians goaltender Chris Clifford became the first goaltender in the history of Canadian Major Junior hockey to score a goal, into an empty-net against the Toronto Marlboros at the Kingston Memorial Centre on January 7, 1986. He went on to play in the NHL with the Chicago Blackhawks.

1988 RECORD LOSING STREAK

Kingston's name was carried to new heights by the township-based Voyageurs. Well-coached by Kevin Abrams, the Vs won the McKenzie Division title and repeated the following year with a pennant-winning effort. The club retired the sweater of Scott Martin, 1985-89, who typified the local player by combining education and hockey. He was named to the division all-star team while netting a record 62 goals and 52 assists for a team-high 114 points. This feat earned him entrance to a college in Rochester, New York.

Kingston Canadians set a league record for the longest losing streak—28 games—including 11 straight at home. It was the worst season in the 15-year history of the franchise as the club finished seventh and dead last in the Leyden Division with only 14 wins. The low point was when the team's new owner, Lou Kazowski, went uninvited behind the bench with coach Jacques Tremblay, who quit in disgust. For the sixth time in the last nine seasons, Kingston finished last in the OHL Leyden.

An AHL pre-season game between Newmarket Saints and Sherbrooke Canadiens attracted 980 fans to the Memorial Centre. The game came on rumours that a Kingston group was investigating the possibility of purchasing an AHL franchise, in case Junior A hockey folded.

Kingston Kodiaks won Ontario Women's Midget B championship under coach Greg Hulse and the captaincy of Dawn Garrett.

Former Kingston Canadian Rob Plumb, after playing in nearly every pro league in North America, completed a seven-year, 218-goal career in the Swiss league. One of his most memorable moments came in the Spengler Cup tournament in 1984. Playing for Canada, Plumb scored with 48 seconds remaining for a 4-3 victory over Soviet Russia. The Canadian goaltender was John Kemp, a former Kingston Canadian. Kemp and Plumb now reside in Battersea, north of Kingston.

1989 LOU, WE HARDLY KNEW YOU

"Real Hockey Is Back in Town," it was announced when local owners of the Kingston Canadians sold out to Peterborough developer Lou Kazowski. He changed the team name to "Raiders" and switched colours from red, white and blue to the black, grey and white of the NFL Oakland Raiders. Despite 25 wins, it was a disturbing and depressing year. His best move was hiring Belleville's Larry Mavety as coach and GM, but the result was the same, a seventh-place finish.

A new club name blossomed in the area when the Kingston Kodiaks, coached by Beth Duff, won one gold, three silvers and a bronze in six women's tournaments. The all-star team from the Frontenac Girls Hockey Association defeated Brampton and

Kingston Canadians Lose 28-Straight Games, 1987-88. Dejected goaltender Franco Giammarco hangs his head following another loss, as the Canadians run up a league record losing streak.

Clearwater and Peterborough at the OWHA Peewee B championship in Mississauga. Kathy VanLuven was the scoring star in the semi-finals, although Jayna Hefford, who grew up in boy's hockey, scored more than one-third of the team's 279 goals during the year. The team was managed by her mother, Sandra Hefford.

The discouraging news on the local front was balanced by the performance of former Kingston players. Doug Gilmour, traded from St. Louis to Calgary, made the Flames burn brighter with 85 points in 72 games and a second overall plus-minus record of 45. He potted 11 goals and as many assists as Calgary skated to its first Stanley Cup. Gilmour scored the game-winning goal in the six-game win over Montreal Canadiens. It duplicated the feat of two other Kingstonians —Ken Linseman, in 1984 when the Edmonton Oilers won their first cup over New York Islanders, and Bill Cook, who scored the only goal in the fourth and deciding game in over-time with Toronto as the New York Rangers captured their second cup in 1933.

Los Angeles Kings' Bernie Nicholls was second only to Mario Lemieux in NHL goal-scoring, tallying 70 in 79 games. For the fourth time, Kirk Muller played for Team Canada at the World Hockey Championships at Stockholm, Sweden, but Canada lost the gold medal game to the Soviets.

Relief and joy came to Kingston in mid-year with the announcement that Wren Blair, former general manager of Kingston's championship EPHL team, and the star of that club, Bobby Attersley, had combined with a third partner to buy the junior franchise and return the name to the traditional one of "Frontenacs."

On the Ontario university front, Ted Linseman had a gala season, leading the Queen's Golden Gaels with19 goals and 26 assists for 45 points in 25 games.

THE LONGEST PLAYOFF GAME

Hockey did an abrupt about-face in the last year of the decade under the revived ownership and the familiar black, gold and white uniforms. And the fans loved their Frontenacs. The all-for-one, one-for-all team chalked up a record 42 victories and missed first place by the slimmest of margins—one point—to Oshawa Generals. The season, however, ended suddenly when the old rivals, Belleville Bulls, won the seventh and deciding playoff game before 3,379 emotionally drained spectators. The Fronts and Bulls played in the longest playoff game (six hours, 16 minutes) in OHL history. It ended with a Belleville goal in the fourth overtime at 1:46 a.m. at the Quinte Sports Centre. Larry Mavety was named the OHL Coach of the Year but he wound up leaving Kingston and returning to the Belleville.

1990

Cup Winning Goal. Doug Gilmour scored the Stanley Cup winning goal at the Montreal Forum in 1989 as the Calgary Flames beat the Canadiens. He is the only player in hockey history to score both a Stanley Cup and Memorial Cup winning goal.

Larry Mavety, OHL Coach of the Year. "Mav" was named the OHL Coach of the Year in 1989-90, having accumulated more than 600 career coaching wins in Kingston and Belleville.

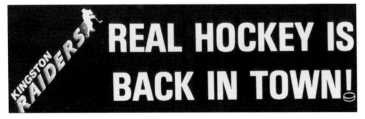

Kingston Raiders, 1988-89. Controversial owner Lou Kazowski purchased the Kingston Canadians and changed their name to "Raiders" for the 1988-89 season. When he threatened to move the team from Kingston the following year, a group headed by Wren Blair and Bob Attersley purchased the club and revived the name "Frontenacs."

Scotty Martin, Kingston Township Voyageurs. The team honoured former star forward Scotty Martin by retiring his Number 10 jersey. A prolific scorer, Scotty's record of 62 goals in a 40 game schedule still stood as a team record in 1989.

Kevin Abrams, Coach, Kingston Township Voyageurs. Now Director of Player Personnel for the Kingston Frontenacs, Kevin had great success coaching the Voyageurs in the late 1980s and early 1990s.

Hockey's *Oldest* Rivalry

The Carr–Harris Cup

"THE CARR-HARRIS CUP . . . brings out the best of what college hockey is all about," Tim Cunningham, Queen's assistant coach, remarked in 2002. Robert Carr-Harris would be pleased and proud to hear this. More than a century after the English-born engineer came to Canada, the double-barrelled family name he created still rings through the rafters of hockey rinks and academic halls. And it perpetuates hockey's oldest rivalry— Royal Military College of Canada versus Queen's University at Kingston.

In 1986 when the International Hockey Hall of Fame and Museum was celebrating the centenary of hockey in Kingston, the directors put forth the Carr-Harris name as a most appropriate one to commemorate the long-standing rivalry between the two institutions. After all, Professor Carr-Harris taught at both RMC and Queen's and many of his eight sons were educated and played hockey for the red and white and tricolour. Their ancestors carried on that tradition into the 20th century. Graduates with the hyphenated "C-H" name dominated the Kingston hockey scene, performed on rinks from Washington to London and served in military and civilian roles from the Klondike and Hong Kong to Egypt and India.

The directors of athletics at the two Kingston schools, Robert D. (Bob) Carnegie and Major (Jim) Gebhardt, both hockey players and still playing the game, picked up the "C-H" puck idea and skated with it. The town-gown-crown organizers soon realized they had a staunch ally for the annual event in Mary Pyke Carr-Harris, widow of John Carr-Harris, who had coached both RMC and Queen's. Her family formed the nucleus of supporters along with that of her brother-in-law, Major Peter Carr-Harris, who confined his coaching to six winters with the senior team at RMC and recorded two victories in West Point against the United States Military Academy.

This gracious, sport-loving Kingston lady, with her deep-rooted family connections, made the annual game a social as well as a sporting success. Not only did her enthusiastic efforts ensure that daughters, sons-in-laws, nieces and nephews from Ottawa to Oakville attended the thrilling contests, but she participated with great delight in opening game ceremonies and post-game presentations.

At face-offs, captains of the Redmen and Golden Gaels doffed their warrior demeanours and in the true style of gentlemen bussed this remarkable lady and returned congratulations. They seemingly endorsed the song, "Mary Is A Grand Old Name" and that "Hockey is a Grand Old Game"—particularly when played by two inter-town rivals with great traditions and respect for their opponents.

Another Kingston woman played an important role in the launching of this unique series. Kingston artist and hockey aficianado Joan Belch created a sculpture of "Lenny," the Queen's player who scored the only goal in the first RMC-Queen's game on Kingston harbour ice in 1886. It was mounted with a rose bowl to become the Carr-Harris Cup.

The gentleman cadets won the inaugural match and the trophy in Constantine Arena. Queen's seemingly turned the series into a rout by winning the next six games. RMC restored the competitive balance by winning three and tying one of the next four contests. Since the cadets adopted the new sobriquet "Paladins" in 1996, the series winner has been a toss-up. The current tally in victories is: Queen's 10, RMC-CMR 6, with one game tied and one game decided in a shoot out.

Originally entitled "The Causeway Challenge" representing the two institutions on each side of the LaSalle Causeway and the Great Cataraqui River, the annual match has been tagged as "The Battle for Kingston" with "bragging rights" to match.

The series has become a spectator bonanza with a little pageantry, duelling bands—both pipe and drums and brass—and partisan cheers. For the most part the action in the stands is tame in comparison to the dash and crash on the ice. "Carr-Harris Hockey" has come to mean intense spirit, endless effort and incredible physical stamina.

"It's the best value for your entertainment dollar—great goaltending, great skating, a ton of hits, 40 shots by each team," said Kevin MacInnis, coach of the, Queen's Golden Gael in 1997. "Don't ask me why, but the Carr-Harris Cup produces exciting hockey."

While Carr-Harris Hockey has brought out accolades for its speed and spirited action, not everyone agrees that that the "war on ice" style of play is a compliment to both institutions. "Hockey is a game of skill combined with talent," wrote Gwen Pooley in 1991. "The Carr-Harris game is an opportunity for these teams to show us this talent. It is not a vendetta of 'civvies' versus 'soldiers.' It should be a game played by talented, educated human beings involved in a friendly rivalry. The desire to play by the rules exhib-

Carr-Harris Cup. An RMC cadet gives Mary Carr-Harris the red carpet treatment at Constantine Arena (top). Accompanied by IHHF President Bill Hamilton, she presents the Carr-Harris Cup to Queen's captains and assistant captains (bottom) during closing ceremonies at Constantine Arena in 1988. Mrs. Carr-Harris has attended all 18 games between RMC and Queen's University.

ited . . . were a disgrace to the name of hockey, its forefathers and spectators. Those guilty should hang their heads in shame."

Obviously a minority opinion, this comment rolls-off the combatants brows as do the beads of sweat from the helmeted and well-padded young board crashers who carry the red and white and the red, blue and old gold colours. They are in the prime of life and they have brought honour to their institutions—and to Carr-Harris family—for their all-out performances over a short but storied 17-year period.

CARR-HARRIS CUP CAUSEWAY CHALLENGE SERIES

Games have been played at Contantine Arena (CA), Jock Harty Arena (JHA), and the Kingston Memorial Centre (KMC).

1986-1987	RMC	8	Queen's	3	Wed., Oct. 22, 1986—CA
1987-1988	Queen's	7	RMC	6	Wed., Oct. 14, 1987—JHA
1988-1989	Queen's	6	RMC	3	Wed., Oct. 12, 1988—KMC
1989-1990	Queen's	11	RMC	4	Wed., Jan. 31, 1990—JHA
1990-1991	Queen's	4	RMC	3	Wed., Jan. 16, 1991—CA
1991-1992	Queen's	7	RMC	2	Wed., Feb. 5, 1992—JHA
1992-1993	Queen's	9	RMC	0	Wed., Feb. 3, 1993—CA
1993-1994	RMC	5	Queen's	2	Sat., Nov. 20, 1993—JHA
1994-1995	RMC*	3	Queen's	3	Fri., Oct. 28, 1994—CA
1995-1996	RMC	2	Queen's	1	Wed., Jan. 10, 1996—JHA
1996-1997	RMC	6	Queen's	5	Wed., Jan. 15, 1997—CA
1997-1998	Queen's	4	RMC	0	Wed., Feb. 11, 1998—JHA
1998-1999	RMC	4	Queen's	3	Wed., Jan. 13, 1999—CA
1999-2000	Queen's	5	RMC	2	Wed., Jan. 12, 2000—JHA
2000-2001	RMC	4	Queen's	2	Wed., Feb. 14, 2001—CA
2001-2002	Queen's	6	RMC	3	Wed., Jan. 16, 2002—JHA
2002-2003	Queen's	3	RMC-CMR	1	Sat., Jan. 25, 2003—CA

Three Top Frontenacs: Keli Corpse, Chris Gratton, Brett Lindros, 1992-93. Kingston Frontenac players were top NHL draft picks (top to bottom): Keli Corpse (2nd round, Montreal), Chris Gratton (1st Round, Tampa Bay), Brett Lindros (1st Round, New York Islanders).

CHAPTER ELEVEN

The No-Win Nineties

What a difference a century makes! Back in the Gay Nineties (1893-1899), when organized hockey was in its infancy, Kingston teams won no less that six provincial titles. One hundred years later, the city's championship hockey record could be labelled: "The Nothing Nineties."

That is, if Joe Fan considers winning everything. The last decade of the 20th century, however, produced much that was positive. The Major Junior hockey franchise was revitalized under an historic name—Frontenacs; the Tier Two Kingston Township Voyageurs had two of their best seasons; women's hockey came into its own; and city sports fans turned their thoughts to honouring the greats of hockey and other sports in the newly created Kingston District Sports Hall of Fame.

Best news of the decade was that the International Hockey Hall of Fame got tentative approval of the International Ice Hockey Federation as its official shrine in North America, thanks to a City of Kingston task force effort under the leadership of Roy B. Conacher and Hockey Canada official, Norm Saunders.

Another Cup Winner. Kirk Muller scored the Stanley Cup winning goal in 1993 as the Montreal Canadiens beat the L.A. Kings.

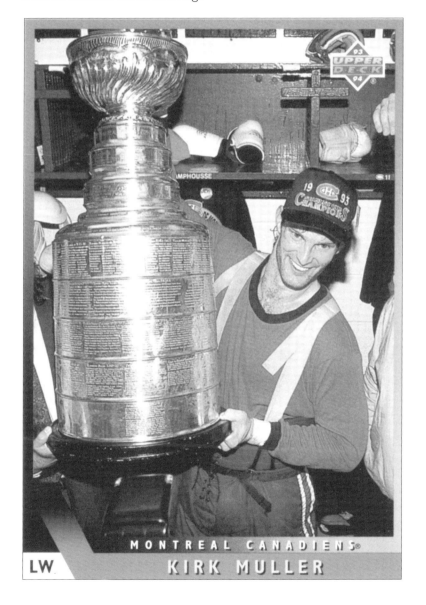

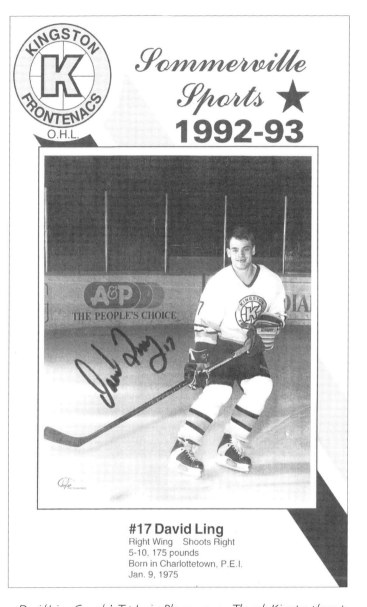

#17 David Ling
Right Wing   Shoots Right
5-10, 175 pounds
Born in Charlottetown, P.E.I.
Jan. 9, 1975

David Ling, Canada's Top Junior Player, 1994-95. The only Kingston player to be named Canada's Top Junior Player following 61-goals and a 135-point season in 1994-95, David was a favorite of the fans.

1991 TOWNSHIPPERS SHOW THE WAY

For the sixth time in the last nine seasons, Kingston finished last in the OHL Leyden Division. It was deeply disappointing for both the Frontenacs and their supporters after the Attersley-Blair combination had turned the franchise around the previous year. New coach Randy Hall was no miracle worker, and the Fronts finished with only 15 wins and four ties. The fans were faithful, however, as average attendance was 2,768.

Peter McGlynn joined Chris Clifford as the second Kingston goaltender to record a goal. On October 11, he scored an empty-netter for Kingston against Belleville Bulls in a 6-4 victory.

Kingston Township brought top honours to the area with a remarkable double championship victory. Patterson Concrete Titans eliminated Bowmanville, Owen Sound and Wexford. They captured the OMHA Midget A crown against Hespeler—the first provincial recognition in the Kingston area in 19 years. To top it, the Titans went on to win the All-Ontario by edging Abitbi, 7-6, thanks to the four-goal effort of winger Darren Hammond. It was a remarkable year for Roy Reid's skaters, winning 43 and tying seven in 65 games. The former Kingston Canadian's assistant coach gave credit to all 15 players under the captaincy of Brian Newton.

1992 KINGSTON TRIO

The Frontenacs, despite a good start under Paul Cook—their third new coach in as many years—ended in their familiar "last-in-the-Leyden" position. One encouraging note was the selection of Chris Gratton—27 goals and 77 points—as the OHL's Rookie of the Year.

Through the Kingston's franchise's name transition, Canadians to Raiders to Frontenacs, three players—Mike Cavanagh, Mike Bodnarchuk and Geoff Schneider—wore three different uniforms.

Queen's and RMC Redmen had seasons that could best be labelled as "character builders." Kingston Township Voyageurs signed affiliation agreements with Ernestown Jets of the Eastern Ontario Junior C League and the Greater Kingston Major Midgets. They came back under the umbrella of the OHA in the Metro Junior B League.

Meanwhile, Kingston's TV viewing fans had much to praise as evident when Eastern Canada's two premier NHL cities, Toronto and Montreal, with centres Doug Gilmour and Kirk Muller, both of Kingston, went head-to-head on CBC's *Hockey Night in Canada*. With hockey's most prominent commentator—Don (Grapes) Cherry—they were saluted as "The Kingston Trio."

Chad Kilger, Kingston Frontenacs, 1993-1995 (right). Anaheim made Kilger the 4th pick overall in the 1995 entry draft. He bounced around with five different NHL teams before finding a home in Montreal following a trade from Edmonton in December 2000.

Craig Rivet, Kingston Frontenacs, 1991-94 (below). A steady stay-at-home defenceman, Rivet has been a regular on the Montreal Canadiens blueline since 1997.

1993

KODIAKS WIN CHAMPIONSHIP

Kingston marked its 20th year in the Major Junior Hockey with a special hockey *Whig-Standard* advertising supplement. Appropriately, the Frontenacs, under coach Dave Allison, won 20 more games than last year, for a total of 36, plus 11 ties for 83 points and second place in the Leyden division. Led by Chris Gratton (55 goals, 109 points), Keli Corpse and Brett Lindros, the team reached the division finals but lost to Peterborough Petes in five games. The Fronts scored 314 goals, the highest since 1981. Ron Brown, the Fronts' marketing man, summed up the previous 19 years without a championship banner as "exciting most of the time, but disappointing more often than rewarding."

A future major leaguer from nearby Gananoque, Alyn McCauley, centring the Voyageurs' hottest line with Chris Gowan and Dan MacKinnon, rolled up a team leading 31 goals and 31 assists in 39 games.

Kingston's Scott Hollis finished an outstanding junior career with Oshawa Generals, topping the 100-point record for the second straight year.

The women showed the way at the Ontario Winter Games at Cornwall, where the Kingston Kodiaks won the Midget A championship, inspired by the offensive power of captain Jayna Hefford and the goaltending of Kelly Reshnyk.

In the NHL, Kirk Muller scored the winning goal as Montreal beat the Los Angeles Kings in the Stanley Cup final, adding his name to that special roll of Kingston cup-winning scorers—Cook, Linseman and Gilmour. Doug Gilmour posted his second 100-point season with Toronto, including a club record of 127 points as the Leafs got within one game of the Stanley Cup final. "Gilly," also known as "Killer" won the NHL's Frank Selke Award for his defensive play.

Another Kingston native, Brandon Convery of the OHL Sudbury Wolves is drafted eighth overall by Toronto. Scott Arniel, mainly a defensive player during a 11-year NHL career, joined the San Diego Gulls of the IHL for the 1992-93 season and put together three consecutive 100-plus point seasons.

1994

LOYAL FANS

The Frontenacs played better than .500 hockey (31-28-8) but only gained the traditional spot: "Fifth in the Leyden." The one bright spot was the impressive play of Keli Corpse, who was elected centre on the second team all-stars. The only scoreless game in Kingston franchise history was telecast from Ottawa by Global TV. Tyler Moss recorded the shutout with 33 stops.

Dave Allison quit as coach/general manager and owner Wren Blair sent him off with a hug and

Matt Bradley, Kingston Frontenacs, 1995-1998. An OHL all-star while playing in Kingston, Bradley was also named the OHL's Most Gentlemanly Player in 1998 and played for Canada at the World Junior Hockey Championships. He began his NHL career with San Jose but was traded to Pittsburgh in March 2003.

Matt Cooke, Kingston Frontenacs, 1997-98. A feisty leftwinger, Cooke made his NHL debut with Vancouver in 1998 and has developed into a valuable role player with the Canucks.

a Frontenac sweater when he emerged five months later as coach of Ottawa Senators' AHL farm team in Prince Edward Island.

The club's inability to mount a super successful season drew editorial comment in *The Whig-Standard*. Veteran journalist Bill Reid noted that the Frontenacs in two decades "hadn't even won a divisional championship, let alone a league title or a berth in the Memorial Cup." But he did have praise for their supporters. "Kingston Junior A hockey fans have turned out to be among the most loyal in the league," he said. "And they're not blindly optimistic. They keep coming back because, by and large, the brand of hockey they've seen—even in losing causes—has been among the best in the country, played by young men who, in many cases, went on to distinguish themselves on the professional circuits."

The restructured Voyageurs, with Chris MacDonald as head coach, compiled a similar record (25-20-3) for fourth in the Bauer division but claimed three individual awards: Kyle Whaley, most valuable player; Matt Donavan, most outstanding defenceman; and Scott Bali, most sportsmanlike player.

The hockey community was saddened by the death of Garry Young, who learned his coaching skills in Kingston and was the first curator of the International Hockey Hall of Fame. The 58-year-old former NHL scout, coach and general manager drowned at his cottage in Haliburton, Ontario.

One year after his Stanley Cup-winning goal and in his first season as captain of the Montreal Canadiens, a tearful Kirk Muller is shocked to learn he has been traded to the New York Islanders. After playing only 27 games, he demands a trade and is eventually traded to Toronto, where he joins captain Doug Gilmour.

Former Kingston forward Darcy Cahill, playing pro in the British league, scored 79 goals and earns 236 points in a 44-game schedule for the Lee-Valley Lions.

1995

A SALUTE TO THE STARS

At the start of the 1994-1995 season, the Frontenacs saluted some of their past stars: Kirk Muller, Bernie Nicholls (63 goals in 1981), Kenny Linseman, (61 goals in 1976), Tony McKegney (58 goals in 1977), Mike O'Connell, Chris Clifford, Chris Gratton and Keli Corpse. They were among the names of 260 players over the past 21 years who were listed in name tags on the cubicle. Head trainer Bob Clarke and assistant Len Coyle, who has been on the job since Day One, affixed the names.

In May 1994, the Frontenacs signed Gary Agnew, a nine-year veteran of the OHL, as coach and general manager. The 34-year-old mentor, who

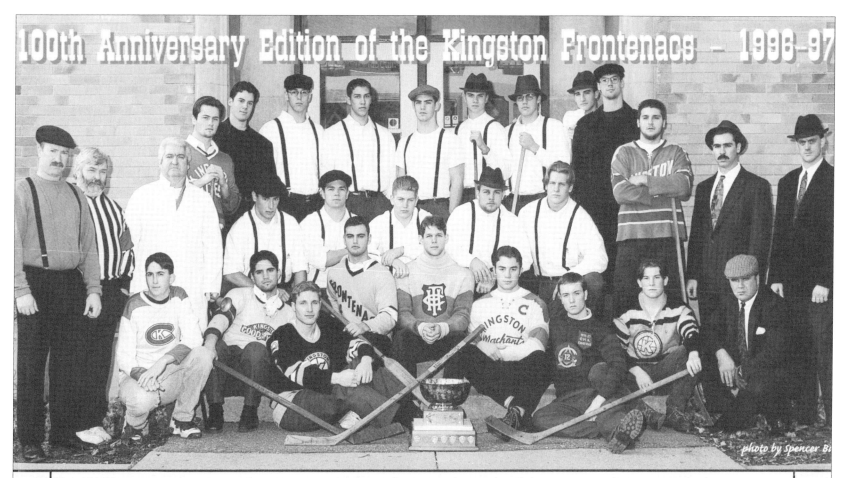

photo by Spencer B...

1896 - 1996
KINGSTON
K
FRONTENACS
100 years

Front row... left to right: Corey Wilson, Mike Oliveira, Roman Malov, Bujar Amidovski, Cail MacLean, Marc Moro (wearing "C"), Mike Laceby, Jason Sands and Shawn Babcock.

Middle row... left to right: Ron St. Clair, Bob Clarke, Len Coyle, Jonathan Schill, Kevin Malcolm, Andre Payette, Mike Tilson, Erik Olsen, Colin Chaulk, Gary Agnew and Chris MacDonald.

Back row ... left to right: Greg Willers, Rob Mailloux, Curtis Cruickshank, Kevin Grimes, Matt Price, Matt Bradley, Aaron Fransen, Justin Davis and Chris Allen.

Special thanks to the International Ice Hockey Federation Museum Inc.

Frontenacs 100th Anniversary. Wearing a collection of old-style Kingston hockey jerseys, the 1996-97 edition of the Kingston Frontenacs celebrated 100-years of Frontenacs hockey.

was 139-107-18 in four seasons with the London Knights, was noted for his people skills and "his ability to communicate with players." The move paid off immediately. The team had a banner year, finishing first behind first team all-stars goaler Tyler Moss, 61-goal scorer and right-winger David Ling and second team all-star defenceman Wes Swinson. They won 40 games, two less than their record 42 wins in 1990, to top the Leyden Division for the first time in history. Ling became the only Frontenac player to be named the top junior hockey player in Canada.

It was a big year for all athletes in Kingston. As a direct result of the Charlie Pester tribute night in 1994, the organizers got together under the leadership of Councillor Joe Hawkins to plan a "Sports Wall of Fame," which became the Kingston and District Sports Hall of Fame in the Kingston Memorial Centre. Spirits and hopes were so high that Kingston bid for the Memorial Cup games.

The Voyageurs, under President Paul Watts with Pat Anson as head coach and Jim Hulton and Rob Blasko as assistants, remained dedicated to developing local talent. The fourth place team gave the touring Central Red Army 1978 born players a stiff battle before their largest crowd of the season, 834 at Cataraqui Arena.

On December 23, Doug Gilmour became the first Kingston-born player to notch 1,000 career points.

Fred J. (Bun) Cook, who died in 1988, was finally inducted into Toronto's Hockey Hall of Fame—22 years after being elected the International Hockey Hall of Fame in his hometown of Kingston.

Jay McKee, a native of Amherstview, was chosen in the first round of the NHL draft by Buffalo Sabres.

1996

V'S TOP TIER TWO

A new spirit reigned at the start of the season as Kingston's mainline team celebrated "100 Years of Frontenac Hockey" and saluted three past stars on opening night: Gary Lavallee (captain of the Junior B Frontenacs), Bob Olajos (of the EPHL Frontenacs) and Gord Harris (of the 1989 team). The Liquor Licensing Board of Ontario allowed the sale of liquor at OHL games, but the Fronts had little need for champagne, finishing fifth and last in the East division with 29 wins in 66 games and 64 points, down 24 from their top spot last season. Insult was added to injury when ex-Kingston Voyageur Scott Cameron, playing with the Peterborough Petes, sunk the Frontenacs.

The first 12 inductees in to the new Kingston sports shrine were three former Kingston juniors—the late Bill Cook, James (Flat) Walsh and Lorne Ferguson who made their names in the NHL.

Kingston Township Voyageurs, 1994-95. A unique team photo taken on the "Spirit of Sir. John A." at Confederation Park. Front row: Scotty Martin Sr. (Asst Mgr), John Thompson (Pres), Rob Blasko (Asst Coach), Pat Anson (Coach), Jim Hulton (Asst Coach), Jack Campbell (Trainer), Hep Lehman (Mgr), Paul Watts (Stats); Middle row: Clint Holmes, Ryan Vivian, Scott Ball, Derek Bowker, Wes Swain, Kevin Dunbar, Derek Melkman, Brent Stevens, Jeff Minnema, Scott Cameron; Back row: Stacey Gregory, Erick James, Corey Crocker, Chris McKeddie, Rob White, Corey Luniman, Martin Boisvenue, Ryan Vince, Tavis Morrison, Jeff Dickson.

In January 1996, Kingston Township Voyageurs were saluted by Ian MacAlpine in a one-page article in *The Whig-Standard* as "one of the top Tier II Junior Hockey Teams in Canada." Ranked as high as second in the nation, the V's outscored the opposition 244-135, won 37 of 50 games and ended a four year playoff drought. President Paul Watts hailed such grads as Kirk Muller, Scott Arniel, Alyn McCauley, Scott Martin, Chris Deruiter, Mike Taylor and Marcel Richard, one of several distinguished players whose skills took him to college hockey in the United States.

Ending a seven-year stint at RMC, Jacques Tremblay is named the CIAU coach of the Year after guiding the Redmen to a play-off spot. Finishing one game below .500, he joined Dave King as the only coach to win the university honour with a team that had a losing record.

Kingston fans were thrilled to see a familiar name "Convery" in hockey headlines. Brandon Convery, son of Kingston Aces' star Charlie Convery, was called up from the AHL St. John's Maple Leafs and scored five goals and earned two assists in 11 games with Toronto's NHL club. The former Kingston Voyageur went on to Vancouver Canucks and Los Angeles Kings and the AHL before finishing his career in Europe.

1997

RYAN VINCE, PLAYER OF THE YEAR

As Kingston opened its 25th season in major junior hockey, changes continued. Gary Agnew—"for the sake of the family"— resigned as coach to return to the London Knights. Larry Mavety sold his 10 per cent share in the Belleville Bulls and started his second stint as coach and general manager here. Chris MacDonald, last year's assistant coach, moved on to the Queen's Golden Gaels.

One of the early games wasn't pretty. "Mav" said the Fronts "look stupid!" Owner Wren Blair was honoured for distinguished service when he received the Bill Long award from the OHL.

Kingston's hockey greats continued to dominate the new inductees in to the city's sports hall of fame, with Bun Cook, Rhonda (Leeman) Taylor and former pro official Art Casterton. Also honoured was veteran broadcaster Max Jackson, who called Kingston Aces' and Kingston Canadians' games.

In September, the sale of 20 per cent of the Frontenacs to Nustadia Developments of Burlington was hailed as the first step to a new rink. "My biggest dream," said owner Wren Blair, "is to drop the puck in a new facility. A new arena is a must for the survival of the junior team."

The Voyageurs put together a banner year under the leadership of captain Ryan Vince, who

Jacques Tremblay, CIAU Coach of the Year. Capping off a seven-year coaching career at RMC, Jacques Tremblay was named the CIAU Coach of the Year in 1996. He joined Dave King as the only other coach to win the prestigious honour coaching a team with a losing record.

Ryan Vince, Kingston Township Voyageurs. Ryan Vince was named the OHA Provincial Junior 'A' player of the year for 1996-97 with 54 goals and a 135-point season. He is now the Voyageurs all-time leading scorer with 155 goals and 337 career points—surpassing Scotty Martin.

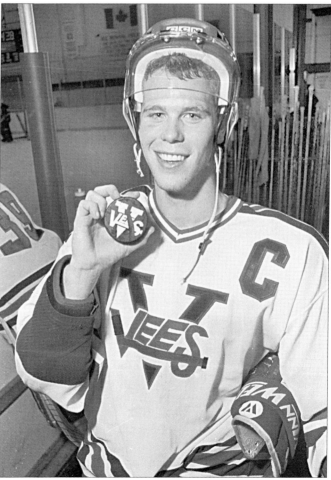

was chosen OHA Provincial Junior A "Player of the Year." Centring a line of Scott Cameron and Rick White, Vince compiled his second consecutive 50-goal seasons with 54, plus 81 assists in 50 games. He became the team's all time leading scorer with most games, 201; most playoff games, 34; most goals, 155; most points 337; and most assists in one season, 81. The "classy, soft-spoken centre" dethroned Scott Martin (296 points) and Cam MacGregor, who set the scoring pace in the late 1980s.

One of the biggest stories of the year was the naming of Kingston's Jayna Hefford to the Canadian Olympic Team. For the 20-year-old winger, who developed her offensive skills in a 10-year career with the Kingston Kodiaks and made the jump to the University of Toronto women's team and the Mississauga Chiefs, it was "a dream come true."

A Dawson City oldtimers' team, who reprised the 4,000-mile trek to challenge Ottawa for the Stanley Cup, detoured to Kingston to duplicate their 1906 visit. Rick Smith, who played for the Ottawa Senators in the highly promoted game before 10,000 people in the nation's capital, suited up, with ex-Bruin Fred O'Donnell in the friendly game against Queen's co-ed team.

Doug Gilmour, one of Toronto's and Kingston's most popular athletes was traded to New Jersey in a deal that included Gananoque's Alyn McCauley

coming to the Leafs. McCauley had finished up a stellar junior career with the Ottawa 67s, earning 112 points and being named the top player in Canadian junior hockey.

"THE BIRD" TAKES FLIGHT

To start the V's silver anniversary year with fourth-year bench coach Pat Anson, the team donned a new name under the sponsorship of Kingston KIMCO Steel Sales and new uniforms.

This was a pivotal year for the Major Junior franchise, then valued above the two million dollar mark. Wren Blair started started the process to sell the Frontenacs to a fifth generation Kingston family. Doug and Michael Springer were to purchase 20 per cent of the shares each year until August 2002 and retain Blair as managing partner. On ice, the Fronts were sparked by Michel "Ziggy" Zigomanis, who compiled 74 points in his rookie year.

The club celebrated 25 years of Major Junior hockey in Kingston with a (1973-1998) logo, a colour poster and an honour roll of 454 players, including three Linsemans—Kenny, Mike and Ted. Chris Allen, following a 28-goal, 94-point season, won the Max Kaminsky Award as the OHL's top defenceman. Teammate Matt Bradley was named the league's most gentlemanly player.

Bryan Allen, a native of Glenburnie, north of

1998

Kingston Kodiaks, Ontario Midget A Champions, Ontario Winter Games, 1993.
The Kodiaks lineup included Jayna Hefford (Captain) and Pam Harvey (Asst Captain).

Kingston Township Midget A OMHA Champions, 1990-91 (top right). Front row: Shawn
Rutledge, Gary Kelly, Darren Hammond, Roy Reid (Coach), Brian Newton, Larry
Hefford (Manager), Roy Adamson, Aaron North, Mike MacPherson; Back row: Bruce
Bogle (Trainer), Mark Thompson, Brendan Rake, Adam Minnion, Scott Manor, Mike
Hefford, Mike Drimmel, Derek Kemp, Alex Brown, Frank Lollar (OMHA Rep), Max
Reddick (Asst Coach).

Kingston Kodiaks, Ontario Champions and Gold Medalists, Canada Winter Games,
1995 (bottom right). Coach Beth Duff, Kelly Sage, Captain Jayna Hefford, Pam Harvey
and Manager Sandra Hefford.

Kingston, was chosen fourth overall in the NHL draft to Vancouver.

Hall of Famer and former MLA, Syl Apps died in Kingston on Christmas Eve after a long illness. The Paris, Ontario native is still remembered and revered in his adopted hometown. At the 1998 Syl Apps Charity Golf Classic, free agent Doug Gilmour agreed by cell phone to a three-year, $18-milllion dollar contract with the Chicago Black Hawks.

CELLAR DWELLERS

There was a new face for a while behind the bench of the Voyageurs. Twenty-nine-year-old Wolfe Islander Jim Hulton came with a reputation as a "fair but demanding coach with a great hockey sense." "Players are at their best," he said at the first media conference, "when they play with emotion and a certain amount of creativity." Mississauga Ice Dogs of the OHL showed more creativity, and before the schedule was 25 games old, stole away Hulton. Pat Anson again picked up the reins.

Cam Kincaid was chosen "defenceman of the year" and Chris Cook celebrated his 17th birthday by scoring seven goals in the final game of the season. This broke the record of six goals in a game held by Scott Martin and Rick White. Cook moved on to the Brampton Battalion, a team that drafted rookie centreman Jay McClement as a replacement for Jason Spezza.

The Frontenacs slipped into their familiar cellar position again, finishing behind Ottawa, Belleville, Oshawa and Peterborough and only garnering more points that Toronto St. Mikes, Mississauga Ice Dogs, and Brampton Battalion, all fairly new franchises.

Gord Wood collected his fourth Memorial Cup ring as a scout with the Ottawa 67s. The long-time scout also helped build Canadian championship teams with three cup victories at Cornwall in 1972, 1980 and 1981.

COOKIE CARTWRIGHT HONOURED

The Voyageurs started their 27th season with 23-year-old Steve Tracze of Belleville, the assistant coach of the Frontenacs, as their newest and youngest coach. The club moved back to Cataraqui Arena from North Frontenac (Picadilly) where all home games "seemed like road games." They finished fifth, ousted Cobourg but couldn't vie for group honours, losing to Lindsay Muskies.

Kingston's Major Junior Frontenac club, in Wren Blair's 11th and last year as major owner, showed marked improvement by winning 38 and tying five for 84 points, the best in five years, to finish third, eight points out of first place. Goaltender

Kingston Red Barons, 1977-78. Kingston's first women's hockey team, in the "modern era," formed in 1969 by Cookie Cartwright and Anabelle Twiddy—both members of the Kingston & District Sports Hall of Fame. The team also included Kim Ferguson, daughter of former NHL'er Lorne Ferguson, who first played on the women's team as a 12-year-old! Front row: Karen Scully, Verna Lee, Wanda Gyde, Carolyn Aylesworth, Cookie Cartwright; Middle row: Eldon Aylesworth (Mgr), Sue McGregor, Carol Pettey, Anabelle Twiddy, Janean Gerow, Lori Boyce; Back row: Linda Murdoch, Kim Ferguson, Janet Fenemore, Bob Weatherdon (Coach).

Andrew Raycroft, drafted by the Boston Bruins, finished his junior career by being named the Canadian Hockey League's outstanding goaltender.

On August 1st, it was announced that Norm Springer and sons Doug and Michael had taken over 60 per cent ownership of the club. Doug immediately announced that the legendary Larry Mavety, "the fourth winningest coach in Canadian junior hockey," who was starting his 19th OHL season, would have 100 per cent control of the franchise. "I want to bring a championship team to this city," said Springer. It was a tall order. At the top team level Kingston hasn't had a major hockey crown in 32 years!

A quarter-century after the fact, Kingston fans wee still talking about the Toronto Marlboros' non-goal that helped eliminate the Canadians from the OHA Junior A play-offs. Mark Napier, who went on to score 235 goals in the NHL, admitted that his shot hit the crossbar and didn't enter the net at the Kingston Memorial Centre.

One of the highlights of the year was the election of Katherine Cartwright to the Kingston and District Sports Hall of Fame. A champion at golf, "Cookie" was a latter-day pioneer in women's hockey. A lawyer in Kingston, she revitalized the game at Queen's University, co-founded the Red Barons hockey team in 1969 and chaired the steering committee that formed the Ontario Women's Hockey Association in 1973.

Her election to the shrine completed a hat trick for women's hockey in Kingston In 1997, Rhonda E. Leeman (Taylor), another Queen's-Red Barons alumni who became the first full-time woman executive in amateur hockey and was later named OWHA regional development co-ordinator, was honoured by the Kingston hall. Their teammate Annabelle Twiddy, a co-founder and "spiritual leader" of the Barons and a star with Queen's, was inducted in 1998.

Kingston's female hockey legacy continued to pay dividends in 2000. Jayna Hefford scored two key goals to help Canada beat the USA and win the gold at the World's Women Hockey Championships.

Jay McKee. Since playing Junior C hockey with the Ernestown Jets, Jay has developed into a solid NHL defenceman with the Buffalo Sabres.

Alan McCauley. A Gananoque native, who played for the Kingston Township Voyageurs as a 14-year-old, Alan broke into the NHL with the Toronto Maple Leafs in 1997 after being named the outstanding player in Canadian junior hockey with the Ottawa 67's.

CHAPTER TWELVE

Years of Hope . . .

Whether Kingstonians celebrated the calendar milestone on January 1, 2000 or January 1, 2001, the new millennium was marked with one four-letter word—"HOPE." Rabid fans, particularly those supporters of the Major Junior Frontenacs, were still hoping for a championship season—even a "finalist" label.

For some hockey buffs, winning isn't everything or the only accomplishment to mark hockey's success in The Limestone City. If participation counts, then hockey on all levels received high marks as the old century finally turned the corner into the new millennium. Women's hockey was to the forefront, the college game was hanging in there, the oldtimers were still sweating and scoring in oldtime fashion and minor hockey, both boys and girls, was bursting the season of seven area rinks.

There was a regular chant for more ice pads, ranging from replacement of the Memorial Centre to the twinning of a neighbour-hood rink. Finally, in 2003, with the International Hockey Museum reverting to its original Hall of Fame name, there was some sign of pay-off for "hope springs eternal." City Council moved ahead with

Jim Hulton and Tony Cimellaro. Wolfe Island native Jim Hulton inspired a sense of optimism when he became coach of the Frontenacs for the 2003-2004 season, joined by assistant coach and former Frontenac player Tony Cimellaro.

KINGSTON FRONTENACS

MIKE ZIGOMANIS ▶ C

Mike Zigomanis, Kingston Frontenacs, 1997-2001. "Ziggy" had 330 points in four seasons with the Frontenacs and made his NHL debut with the Carolina Hurricanes during the 2002-03 NHL season.

plans to twin the 33-year-old Centre 70 in the Reddendale section of the former Kingston Township, and Queen's University announced an ambitious multi-million expansion of physical education facilities to include a 3,500 seat multi-purpose centre with regulation ice surface.

The cheers could be heard throughout the town, even as some jeered the fact that the old Wally Elmer and Cook Brothers arenas, along with the other work-horses of inner city rinks, including the Harold Harvey arenas, weren't included in immediate plans for updating and renovations. But there was a glimmer of hope in the late spring announcement of the Ontario government that Kingston had qualified for a $600,000 grant under the Super Build program.

2001 HOPE "SPRING(ER)S" ETERNAL

The Frontenacs, with the Springer family in a majority ownership position, came out with a new look in the middle of the season—a third jersey with a cartoon–styled Count Frontenac crest in place of the traditional "K," and the addition of a new colour silver to go with gold, black and white. After going undefeated in eight straight home games, the "Mavetymen" weren't so inspiring in their new dress. They played exactly .500 hockey (28-28-11) for 68 points in 68 games and fourth place.

The Voyageurs compiled a respectable 25-win season under four-year veteran Andrew (Hause) Haussler, who served as captain. They eliminated Peterborough in six games but fell four straight to Lindsay. Off the ice it was a sad season—losing their coaching staff and sponsor. Reportedly $34,000 in the hole, the club was rife with "personality conflicts" and announced a "house cleaning."

In OHL news, Don Cherry shocked the hockey worlds by returning behind the bench to coach the OHL's Mississauga Ice Dogs. The OHL team, which he helped form and finance, won just 11 games and missed the play-offs—again. Cherry quit and then retained his CBC commentating job.

In 2001, Doug Gilmour hinted about retirement after 18 NHL seasons as he left Buffalo Sabres but he went on to join the Montreal Canadiens.

2002 HEFFORD BRINGS HOME GOLD

This season was highlighted by Kingston's Jayna Hefford scoring the winning goal in the gold medal game against the United States at the Salt Lake City Olympics. Tallied on an individual effort with one second to go in the second period, this spectacular goal gave Canada a two-goal cushion and the championship. It added to her long list of laurels, including two world's gold medals, an Olympic

Olympic Gold Winning Goal. Jayna Hefford (left) shows off her gold medal following her game-winning goal in the championship game at the 2002 Olympics in Salt Lake City.

silver medal, a MVP award in the National Women's League in 2001 and Canada's leading scorer in the 1999 World's tournament.

For the Frontenacs, it was back to "fifth in the east" as the local club was held to only 22 wins. Mavs' men outscored five other teams but couldn't keep the puck out of the net. They gave up 320 goals, third only to the new franchises of Brampton and Mississauga.

In just his third professional game in goal, 20-year-old Verona native Mike Smith scored a goal and posted a shutout for Lexington, Kentucky Men O'War in an East Coast Hockey League game against the Dayton Bombers. "It's pretty cool to have a record," says the youngest goaltender to score a goal at the pro level. "I don't think I'll have too many in my career."

Scott Arniel, who spent part of his 730-game NHL career with the Buffalo Sabres, returned to the team as an assistant coach.

2003

HULTON'S HIGH HOPES

Hopes were high for this season, but it was the old story and a familiar spot for the Frontenacs—fifth and last in the east. The team won only 25 of 68 games and finished the season with six consecutive losses. It was a disappointing season for the Springer family and for coach Greg Bignell, who took over bench duties from Larry Mavety and compiled a 15-20-2 record.

Optimism took a sudden surge in April when the Fronts announced that Wolfe Island's Jim Hulton was coming home to coach the Kingston club for the 2003-2004 season. The former Belleville Bulls and Mississauga Ice Dogs mentor was introduced as the 15th coach in Kingston's 30-year franchise history. His bywords: "Hard work and commitment." He earned his spurs in the OHL and was accorded the high honour of being named coach of Team Canada's under-18 team that won the gold medal. Also adding to the optimism was the first-round draft pick of the Frontenacs—Tony Rizzi, "a character player" with the Wellington Dukes.

Women's hockey got an unexpected boost with the word that ex-Kingstonians Laura Hurd, Liz Gibson and Lisa Bettencourt set standards in U.S. college hockey. Hurd registered 33 goals and 51 points with the Elmira (New York) College Eagles and was selected as a first team all-star. Gibson, a Holy Cross grad, collected 69 points in 22 games in her freshman season with Plattsburg State University Cardinals and was selected as "rookie of the year." Teammate Lisa Bettencourt, also a Holy Cross grad, garnered 45 points over two seasons of playing forward and defence and ranked fifth in career team scoring.

Kirk Muller and Doug Gilmour Retire. After a 19-year NHL career, Kirk Muller announced his retirement in September 2003 at the International Hockey Hall of Fame. One week later, Doug Gilmour called it quits following a 20-year pro career.

Kingston's contribution to hockey in other cities was emphasized by the appointment of Marty Abrams as head coach of the Sault Ste. Marie Greyhounds of the Ontario Hockey League. Abrams had recently coached the Wellington Dukes to the 2003 Tier II final four in Prince Edward Island, had served as head scout of the Kingston Frontenacs for two seasons, and had stopped pucks for the Canadian Soo team that earned an OHL title in 1984-85.

To prove that there are few hockey games played without a Kingston connection, the Vancouver Canucks made their Stanley Cup bid with the help of the stirring play of Matt Cooke, a former Frontenac. Another Limestone City grad who started his career as a 15-year-old with the Junior A Canadians was Kirk Muller. The veteran centre potted a vitally important goal as the Dallas Stars battled for survival against the Anaheim Mighty Ducks. Also playing a support role with the Buffalo Sabres was Jay McKee, a solid two-way defenceman.

While Kingston's favourite NHL star, Doug Gilmour, had to sit out Toronto Maple Leafs' playoff action because of an injury, his fervent supporter Don Cherry was extolling the merits of all Kingston hockey talent on CBC's *Hockey Night in Canada*. The strident voice of Coaches Corner, who grew up a slapshot away from the Memorial Centre,

has tempered his "Kingston First" proclamations somewhat, but he can still be counted on to remind hockey fans that there is no better producer of talent than the Limestone City. To confirm this, one only has to review *The Cradle of Hockey* roster of the many Kingstonians in the NHL as dutifully compiled by former Frontenac information officer Jeff Stilwell.

As the 118th Kingston hockey season—2003-2004—approached the 53-year-old Memorial Centre, dismissed by a Queen's academic as "decrepit," got a new roof. And there was news that a new level of competition might return to the ice lanes. A Senior A league, featuring teams from Belleville, Cobourg, Prescott, Deseronto, Tamworth and Kingston, was in the discussion stage. Could the Kingston Aces rise from the ashes of 1972? Could be! Kingston started out in senior hockey in 1891. There may not be a Guy Curtis or a Jock Harty around or a Bill Burega or a Ron Earl barrelling up the ice to challenge for the Allan Cup, but there could be a squad of young men who love the thrills of the game so much they'd even pay to play. Stay tuned! Hope and Heart are bywords of Kingston's hockey heritage—as epitomized by Captain Sutherland!

Coach's Corner: Ron McLean and Don Cherry. Whig-Standard *cartoonist Frank Edwards asks:* "Guess which one boosts Kingston?"

The Cradle *of* Hockey

National Hockey League Players From Kingston

	GP	G	A	PTS.
GEORGE ABBOTT				
b. Aug 03 1911, Sydenham, ON				
1943-44: Boston	1	0	0	0
BRYAN ALLEN				
b. 21 Aug 1980, Kingston				
2000-2003: Vancouver	65	5	3	8
Playoffs	3	0	0	0
SYL APPS SR.				
b. 18 Jan 1915, Paris, ON				
d. 24 Dec 1998, Kingston				
1936-48: Toronto	423	201	231	432
Playoffs	69	25	29	54

OVER THE PAST 100 YEARS, Kingston, Ontario has been called "Hockey's Home" and, erroneously, "The Birthplace of Hockey," but it can truthfully vie for the honour of the title of "The Cradle of Hockey." Jeff Stilwell, former marketing manager for the Kingston OHL Frontenacs, researched and compiled this report in 2002. Mark Potter has updated the statistics to the end of the 2002-2003 season and added additional players to the list.

Jeff set two criteria – 1: Born in Kingston and /or 2: Kingston played a role in their life, before, during or after their NHL career finished. The list includes players who were not born here but call Kingston home. We've taken the liberty of adding Gary MacGregor, who starred in the WHA, and Wally Elmer, a Stanley Cup winner with Victoria, who never played in the NHL but made a valuable contribution to the game in Kingston. Other candidates are Hall of Famers Allan (Scotty) Davidson and George T. Richardson, plus Art Bernier, all of whom were prominent before the NHL was formed.

Sixty-six players (and counting) with ties to Kingston have played in the NHL. Of course, there are many more players not included who played their junior hockey in Kingston or played here professionally with the EPHL Frontenacs.

	GP	G	A	PTS.
SYL APPS, JR.				
b. 01 Aug 1947, Toronto				
1970-1980: Pittsburgh, L.A.,	727	183	423	606
New York Rangers Playoffs	23	5	5	10
SCOTT ARNIEL				
b. 17 Sept 1962, Kingston				
1982-92: Winnpeg, Buffalo,	730	149	189	338
Boston Playoffs	34	3	3	6
MICKEY BLAKE				
b. 31 Oct 1912, Barriefield				
1932-36: Montreal Maroons,	10	1	1	2
St Louis Eagles, Toronto				

Mickey Blake

	GP	G	A	PTS.
CAM BOTTING				
b. 10 Mar 1954, Kingston				
1975-76: Atlanta	2	0	1	1
KIP BRENNAN				
b. 27 Aug 1980, Kingston				
2001-02: L.A	4	0	0	0
FRED (BALDY) BROWN				
b. 15 Sept 1900, Kingston				
1927-28: Montreal Maroons	19	1	0	1
ROB BROWN				
b. 10 Apr 1968, Kingston				
1987–2000: Pittsburgh,				
Hartford, Chicago,.	543	190	248	438
L.A., Dallas Playoffs	54	12	14	26
JACK CAFFERY				
b. 30 June 1934, Kingston				
1954-58: Toronto, Boston	57	3	2	5
Playoffs	10	1	0	1
WAYNE CASHMAN				
b. 24 June 1945, Kingston				
1964-1983: Boston	1,027	277	516	793
Playoffs	145	31	57	88
DON CHERRY				
b. 05 Feb 1934, Kingston				
1954-55: Boston	0	0	0	0
Playoffs	1	0	0	0

**DICK CHERRY
FLYERS**

	GP	G	A	PTS.
DICK CHERRY				
b. 28 Mar 1937, Kingston				
1956-70: Boston, Philadelphia	145	12	10	22
Playoffs	4	1	0	1
TONY CIMELLARO				
b. 14 June 1971, Kingston				
1992-93: Ottawa	2	0	0	0
BRANDON CONVERY				
b. 14 Feb 1974, Kingston				
1995-99: Toronto, Vancouver	72	9	19	28
Playoffs	5	0	0	0
ALEXANDER (BUD) COOK				
b. 15 Nov 1907, Kingston				
d. 13 Nov 1993				
1931-1934: Boston, Ottawa	50	5	4	9

	GP	G	A	PTS.
FRED (BUN) COOK				
b. 18 Sept 1903, Kingston,				
d. 19 Mar 1988				
1926-37: New York Rangers, Boston	473	158	144	302
Playoffs	46	15	3	18
WILLIAM (BILL) COOK				
b. 08 Oct 1895, Brantford				
d. 06 Apr 1986				
1926-1937: New York Rangers	474	229	138	367
Playoffs	46	13	11	24
PETER DINEEN				
b. 19 Nov 1960, Kingston				
1986-1990: L.A., Detroit	13	0	2	2
JIM DOREY				
b. 17 Aug 1947, Kingston				
1968-72: NHL: Toronto,				
New York Rangers	232	25	74	99
Playoffs	11	0	2	2
1972-79: WHA: New England,				
Toronto, Quebec	431	52	232	284
Playoffs	51	5	33	38
WALLY ELMER				
b. 1898, Kingston				
d. 28 Aug 1978				
1922-29: WCHL, CPHL, CAHL	114	18	14	32
JOHN ERSKINE				
b. 26 June 1980, Kingston				
2001-2003: Dallas Stars	49	2	1	3
SHAWN EVANS				
b. 07 Sept 1965, Kingston				
1985-90: St. Louis, New York Islanders	9	1	0	1

	GP	G	A	PTS.
LORNE FERGUSON				
b. 26 May 1930, Palmerston, ON				
1950-59: Boston, Detroit, Chicago	422	82	80	162
Playoffs	31	6	3	9
ALEX FORSYTH				
b. 06 Jan 1955, Galt, ON				
1976-77: Washington	1	0	0	0
DOUG GILMOUR				
b. 25 June 1963, Kingston				
1983-2003: St. Louis, Calgary,				
Toronto, New Jersey, Chicago,				
Buffalo, Montreal	1474	450	964	1414
Playoffs	182	60	128	188
HANK GOLDUP				
b. 29 Oct 1918, Kingston				
1939-46: Toronto,				
New York Rangers	202	63	80	143
Playoffs	26	5	1	6
ROD GRAHAM				
b. 19 Aug 1946, London, ON				
1974-75: Boston	14	2	1	3
TODD HAWKINS				
b. 2 Aug 1966, Kingston				
1988-1992: Vancouver, Toronto	10	0	0	0
JAKE HENDRICKSON				
b. 05 Dec 1936, Kingston				
1958-62: Detroit	5	0	0	0
DENNIS KEARNS				
b. 27 Sept 1945, Kingston				
1971-81: Vancouver	677	31	290	321
Playoffs	11	1	2	3

	GP	G	A	PTS.
NICK KNOTT				
b. 23 July 1920, Kingston				
d. 12 Apr 12, 1987				
1941-42: Brooklyn Americans	14	3	1	4
GUY LEVEQUE				
b. 28 December 1972, Kingston				
1992-94: L.A.	17	2	2	4
KEN LINSEMAN				
b. 11 Aug 1968, Kingston				
1978-92: NHL: Philadelphia,				
Edmonton,	860	256	551	807
Boston, Toronto Playoffs	114	43	77	120
1977-78: WHA, Birmingham	71	38	38	76
Playoffs	5	2	2	4
GARY MACGREGOR				
b. 21 Sept 1954, Kingston				
d. 20 Apr 1995				
1974-79: WHA: Chicago,				
New England, Denver,	251	90	70	160
Indianapolis, Ottawa,				
Cleveland Playoffs	3	0	0	0
ALYN MCCAULEY				
b. 29 May 29 1977, Brockville, ON				
1996-2003: Toronto, San Jose	320	36	56	92
Playoffs	35	5	10	15
JAY MCKEE				
b. 8 Sept 1977, Kingston				
1996-2003: Buffalo	464	10	67	77
Playoffs	34	1	3	4
MIKE MEEKER				
b. 23 Feb 1958, Kingston				
1978-79: Pittsburgh	4	0	0	0

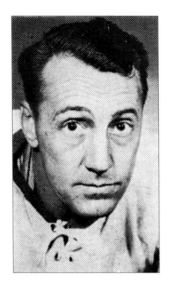
Ted Nicholson

Fred O'Donnell

FRED O'DONNELL

1973 - 1974

	GP	G	A	PTS.
KIRK MULLER				
b. 08 Feb 1966, Kingston				
1984-2003: New Jersey, Montreal,				
NY Islanders, Toronto Florida,				
Dallas	1349	357	602	959
Playoffs	127	33	36	69
MIKE MURRAY				
29 Aug 1966, Kingston				
1987-88: Philadelphia	1	0	0	0
ROBERT (BOB) MURRAY				
b. 26 Nov 1954, Kingston				
1975-90: Chicago	1,008	132	382	514
Playoffs	112	19	37	56
EDWARD (TED) NICHOLSON				
1947-48: Detroit	1	0	0	0
FRED O'DONNELL				
b. 06 Dec 1949, Kingston.				
1971-1974: NHL: Boston	115	15	11	26
Playoffs	5	0	1	1
1974-76 WHA: New England	155	32	26	58
Playoffs	20	2	5	7
DON O'DONOGHUE				
b. 27 Aug 1949, Kingston				
1969-72: NHL: Oakland/California	125	18	17	35
Playoffs	3	0	0	0
1972-76: WHA: Philadelphia,				
Vancouver, Cincinnati	147	25	37	62
Playoffs	4	0	1	1
RICK PATERSON				
b. 10 Feb 1958, Kingston				
1978-1987: Chicago	430	50	43	93
Playoffs	61	7	10	17

	GP	G	A	PTS.
GEORGE (PADDY) PATTERSON b. 22 May 1906, Kingston d. 20 Jan 1977 1926-35: Toronto, Montreal, NY Americans				
Boston, Detroit, St. Louis Eagles	284	51	27	78
Playoffs	3	0	0	0
ROB PLUMB b. 29 Aug 1957, Kingston				
1977-79: Detroit	14	3	2	5
RON PLUMB b. 17 July 1950, Kingston				
1979-80: NHL: Hartford	26	3	4	7
1972-79: WHA: Philadelphia, Vancouver, San Diego,	549	65	264	329
Cincinnati, New England Playoffs	41	5	15	20
KEN RANDALL b. 14 Dec 1888, Kingston/ Watertown, NY				
1919-1927: Toronto St. Pat's,	217	67	28	95
Hamilton Tigers, NY Americans				
BRIT SELBY b. 27 Mar 1945, Kingston				
1964-72: NHL: Toronto, Vancouver,	347	55	62	117
Philadelphia, St. Louis. Playoffs	16	1	1	2
1972-75: WHA: Quebec, New England, Toronto	153	23	51	74
Playoffs	23	4	7	11
RICK SMITH b. 29 June 1948, Kingston				
1968-1981: NHL: Boston, Detroit, Washington	687	52	167	219
Playoffs	78	3	23	26
1973-76: WHA: Minnesota	200	20	89	109
Playoffs	23	2	8	10

	GP	G	A	PTS.
TREVOR STIENBURG b. 13 May 1966, Kingston				
1985-89: Quebec	71	8	4	12
ANDY SUTTON b. 10 Mar 1975, Kingston 1998-2003: San Jose,				
Minnesota, Atlanta	236	9	34	43
TOM THURLBY b. 09 Nov 1938, Kingston				
1967-68: Oakland	20	1	2	3
JOHN TRIPP b. 04 May 1977, Kingston				
2002-2003: NY Rangers	9	1	2	3
RIK WILSON b. 17 June 1962, Long Beach, CA 1981-1988: St. Louis, Calgary,				
Chicago	251	25	65	90
Playoffs	22	0	4	4

GOALTENDERS

	GP	W	L	T	GAA
CHRIS CLIFFORD b. 26 May 1966, Kingston					
1984-88: Chicago	2	0	0	0	0.00
MIKE MOFFATT b. 26 May 1966, Galt, ON					
1981-83: Boston	19	7	7	2	4.29
Playoffs	11	6	5	0	3.43

Les Douglas

Joe Levandoski

CHARLES E. (DOC) STEWART
b. 13 Nov 1895, Carleton Place, ON
d. Nov 1972

	GP	G	A		
1924-27: Boston	77	30	41	5	2.45

W.J (BILL) TAUGHER
b. 1907, Kingston
d. 25 Feb 1943

	GP	G	A		
1925-26: Montreal	1	0	1	0	n/a

JAMES (FLAT) WALSH
b. 23 Mar 1897, Kingston
d. 02 Dec 1959

		GP	G	A		
1926-1933: Montreal Maroons,		108	48	43	16	2.31
NY Americans	Playoffs	8	2	4	2	1.68

NHL PLAYERS WHO FINISHED THEIR CAREERS IN KINGSTON:

	GP	G	A	PTS.
BILL BUREGA b. 01 May 1932, Winnipeg				
1955-56: Toronto	4	0	1	1
LES DOUGLAS b. 05 Dec 1918, Perth, ON d. 20 Oct 2002, Kingston				
1940-47: Detroit	52	6	12	18
Playoffs	10	3	2	5

	GP	G	A	PTS.
JOE LEVANDOSKI b. 17 Mar 1921, Cobalt, ON d. 20 Dec 2001, Kingston				
1946-47: NY Rangers	8	1	1	2
HUB MACEY b. 13 Apr 1921, Big River, SK				
1941-47: Montreal, NY Rangers	30	6	9	15
GUS MARKER b. 01 Aug 1907, Wetaskawin, AB d. 07 Oct 1997, Kingston 1932-1942: Detroit, Montreal Maroons, Toronto,				
Brooklyn Americans	336	64	69	133
Playoffs	35	4	6	10
HARRY (YIP) RADLEY b. 27 June 1908, Ottawa d. 19 Aug 1963, Kingston 1930-37: NY Americans,				
Montreal Maroons	19	0	1	1

Hockey Hall of Fame
Kingston, Canada

IHHFM Directors

1943–2003

OVER SIX DECADES, THE International Hockey Hall of Fame and Museum has been directed by a large group of volunteers—some-short term, some serving for decades, but representing a cross-section of the academic, business, professional and sporting communities of Kingston. They have served under the leadership of devoted presidents and under the shield of a variety of Hall of Fame logos. All were dedicated to preserving and promoting the city and district's rich hockey heritage.

Here they are, listed alphabetically, with presidents marked with an asterisk*:

R.H. (Bud) Aitken
R.M. Allan
Al Allmark
Thomas A. Andre
W.S. (Wally) Avis

Don Bearss
R.G. Beck
C.O. Boak
Don Boswell
C.L. Boyd

Bill Burega
Edwin Bryce
*Brian Bunting

Andre Cantin
R.D. (Bob) Carnegie
John Carr-Harris
Russell Carter
Art Casterton
J.A. Casterton
William Casey

Edward W. Charlton
D.H. (Doug) Clark
John Clements
*Roy B. Conacher
Fred J. (Bun) Cook
Lorne A. Cook
William O. Cook
W.T. (Jim) Cook
Cecil C. Cornelius
W.J. (Jack) Crawford
Reg Crawford
*J. Stuart Crawford
*William Crews
Wayne Crossen
Brig. B.G. Cunningham
E.G. (Ted) Cuthbert
Joe Daley
William Dodd

Cliff Earl
W.D. (Wally) Elmer

Col. A.H. Fair
Rev. L.J. Fischer
*J.W. (Bill) Fitsell
C.C. Folger
Douglas Ford
Edward (Ted) Fowler
Ed Friel
Douglas Fluhrer

Lorne (Curly) Gallivan
Gil Gardner
*James B. Garvin
John B. Garvin
Lt. Col. T.F. Gelley

Sy Golosky
T.E. (Tom) Gray
*Edward R. Grenda

*Bill Hamilton
*E.H. (Ebby) Hare
*Fred Harkness
James Harris
Harold Harvey
Neil Hay
Don Haylock
Clare Henderson
William J. Henderson
R.G. (Bob) Hickeson
Paul Hoag
Ed Hogan
W.P.R. Holdcroft
Ed Hulse
Herb Hunter
Elmer Hurlbut
Mel Hutchinson

Lt. Col. Isbister

Max Jackson
A.J. Jarvis

William Kelly
Howard Keyes
Thomas Kirby
*Wayne Kirk
Bill Kirkpatrick

J.A.L. (Leo) LaFleur
*Aime (Joe) Lalonde
Harold Langabeer

Geof R. Lauer	*Douglas B. Nichols	Bill Richmond	
	Josh Nichols	Michael J. Rodden	Major Tanner
Hub Macey	Wayne Nichols		Herb Thomson
Dave McLaren	William F. Nickle	*Norm Saunders	R.G.H. Travers
Gus Marker		Douglas Slater	Jacques Tremblay
J. McGee	Larry Paquette	David Sleeth	
T.A. McGinnis	*Mark Potter	Alistair N. Smith	James P. (Flat) Walsh
W.J. (Danny) McLeod	Frank Purdy	Harry P. Smith	William J. Walshe
H.A. McNeill		Murray Smith	Ted Walton
Nels D. Megaffin	Phil Quattrocchi	Herb Steacy	Steve Watt
R.F. Millan		B. Noble Steacy	G.E. (Gerry) Watters
G.R. (Doc) Myles	Peter J. Radley	William Steacy	Ed Watts
J.L. Murray	Bill Reason, Jr.	Harry A. Stewart	George Webb
	Melville J. (Star) Reid	E.J. Squires	Ross Wotten
Lt. Col. P.T. (Pit) Nation	James D. St. Remy	Capt. James T. Sutherland	*William G. Watts

International Hockey Hall of Fame Directors, 1996-97. Left to right: Bill Fitsell, Ed Grenda, Sy Golosky, Mark Potter, Roy B. Conacher, Don Haylock, Wayne Kirk, Fred Harkness, Aime Lalonde and Andre Cantin kneel before the International Ice Hockey Federation exhibit.

Max Jackson, Kingston & District Sports Hall of Fame, 1997. Longtime CKWS Sports Director was the play-by-play voice of the Kingston Aces and Kingston Canadians.

Bill Reason, Kingston & District Sports Hall of Fame, 2000. Involved in Kingston hockey for 50 years, Bill enjoyed success as a coach, executive, referee and NHL scout.

Bob Senior, Kingston & District Sports Hall of Fame, 2001. A goaltender who won a Memorial Cup with the 1956 Toronto Marlboros, Bob later coached both the Jr B Frontenacs and the Kingston Township Voyageurs.

Bill Burega, Kingston & District Sports Hall of Fame, 2002. Player with the Kingston Aces Senior A teams in the 1960s.

Ron Earl, Kingston & District Sports Hall of Fame, 2001. Player with the Kingston Aces Senior A teams in the 1960s.

Tom Carty, Kingston & District Sports Hall of Fame, 1999. Player with the Kingston Aces Senior A teams in the 1960s.

Acknowledgements

"A team" was responsible for producing this book.

First and foremost, thanks must go to Mark Potter, who has almost single-handedly sparked the revival of the International Hockey Hall of Fame in the 21st Century. He seized on the idea of marking the Hall's 60th anniversary with a record of Kingston's rich hockey past and contributed markedly to the updating and editing.

To colleague Doug Ford for technical support and the encouragement and advice of other fellow board directors, Roy B. Conacher, Lorne Gallivan, Sy Golosky, Ed Grenda and Larry Paquette, goes my sincere appreciation.

We are all especially grateful to Bob Hilderley for providing his expert advice in various stages of planning and producing the manuscript, and to Laura Brady for her graphic design skills.

The efforts of Ernie and Marlene Fitzsimmons of Fredericton, N.B. and Chris Peck of Med Photo, who scanned many of the fine images in the book, are applauded and much appreciated.

Kudos also go to the many people who loaned or donated photographs and images and provided information, including Jim Gilchrist Roy (Scotty) Martin, Roy Reid, Brian and Sandra Roe, Charles and Connie Wiskin and Randy Genois. And I thank James M. Chapeskie, the Poet of the People and the Puck, for permission to reproduce his Kingston hockey centennial poem, *The Puck Is Dropped*.

The Kingston story would not have told without the statistical contribution of Jeff Stilwell and his *"Cradle of Hockey"* feature.

Special mention must be made of the contribution of Kingston photographer Bernard Clark who was specially commissioned to take colour photographs of special exhibits. The camera excellence of Wallace R.Berry is also recorded here. Thank you!

This project would not have been launched without the approval and generous support of *The Kingston Whig-Standard*, publisher Fred LaFlamme, sports editor Claude Scilley and photographer Ian McAlpine. Former Whig photographers Bill Baird and the late Cliff Knapp and Bill O'Neill also have their work shining forth.

Above all, *Hockey's Hub* would not have been financially feasible without the generous grants of the City of Kingston's Healthy Community Fund and the Davies Foundation. We are indeed most grateful.

Last but not least, we salute all hockey fans that have made Kingston an exemplary hockey city—one worth recording and remembering.

—J.W. (BILL) FITSELL